VIRGINIA

VIRGINIA BY ROAD

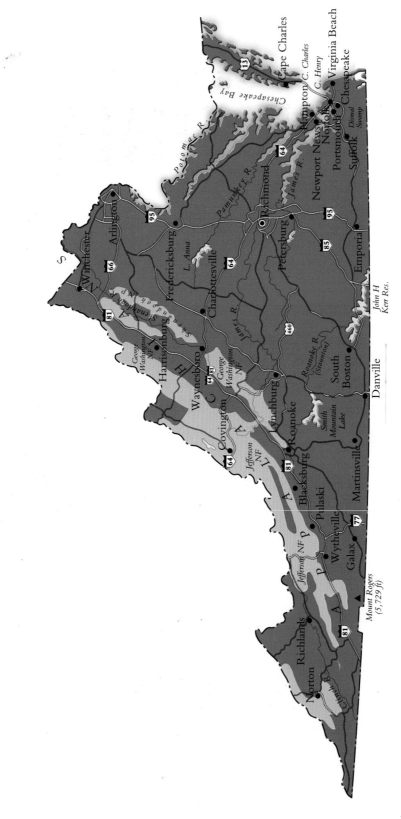

CELEBRATE THE STATES
VIRGINIA

Tracy Barrett

BENCHMARK BOOKS

MARSHALL CAVENDISH
NEW YORK

For Greg, Laura Beth, and Patrick

Benchmark Books
Marshall Cavendish Corporation
99 White Plains Road
Tarrytown, New York 10591-9001

Library of Congress Cataloging-in-Publication Data
Barrett, Tracy, date
Virginia / by Tracy Barrett.
p.   cm. —.(Celebrate the states)
Includes indexes.
Summary: Surveys the geography, history, economy, and people of the state of Virginia.
ISBN: 0-7614-0110-5 (lib. Bdg.)
1. Virginia—Juvenile literature. [1. Virginia.] I. Title. II. Series
F226.3.B35   1997   975.5—dc20   96-12972   CIP   AC

Maps and Graphics supplied by Oxford Cartographers, Oxford, England

Photo research by Matthew Dudley

Cover photo: *The Image Bank*, Gary Cralle

The photographs in this book are used by permission and through the courtesy of: *The Image Bank:* Pamela Zilly, 6-7, 17; Timothy A. Murphy, 10-11; David W. Hamilton, 13; John Lewis Stage, 22, 77, 135; Gary Cralle, 48-49; Marvin E. Newman, 64-65; Kay Chernush, 69; Lisa J. Goodman, 96-97, 134; Murray Alcosser, 112; Michael R. Schneps, back cover. *Virginia Division of Tourism:* 15, 88. *William B. Folsom:* 20, 40, 104, 115, 123. *Virginia Museum of Fine Arts, Richmond, VA, The Paul Mellon Collection:* 24-25. *Corbis-Bettmann:* 27, 31, 32, 33, 35 (right), 35 (left), 37, 39, 54, 83, 85, 128, 131. *Jackson Davis Collection, Special Collection Dept., University of Virginia Library:* 45. *UPI/Corbis-Bettman:* 55, 89, 126 (right), 129, 130. *Robert Llewellyn:* 56, 100. *Photo Researchers, Inc.:* Kenneth Murray, 59, 79; Jim Amos, 62; Chromosohm/Sohm, 67; Lee Bataglia, 79; Rita Nannini, 80-81; Brian Hemphill, 86; Jack Fields, 94; Farrell Grehan, 103; William H. Mullins, 107; George Chan, 108; Jeff Greenberg, 114; Stephen J. Kraseman, 117 (right); Arvil A. Daniels, 117 (left), Jeff Lapore, 120 (right); Lynda Richardson, 120 (left); Richard T. Nowitz, 137. *Beth Ahabah Museum and Archive:* 72. *Reuters/Corbis-Bettmann:* 92, 126 (left). *Peter Arnold, Inc./Lynda Richardson:* 120 (left). *Springer/Corbis-Bettman:* 127.

Printed in Italy

3   5   6   4

CONTENTS

INTRODUCTION   VIRGINIA IS . . .   6

1 GEOGRAPHY   "A GLORIOUS PARADISE"   10
MANY VIRGINIAS • A PLEASANT CLIMATE AND BEAUTIFUL BIRDS • "THE
GREATEST PEOPLE IN THE WORLD"

2 HISTORY   THE COLONIE OF VIRGINIA   24
THE JAMESTOWN SETTLEMENT • THE WESTWARD PUSH • "AN INHUMAN
PRACTICE" • SONG: "ALL QUIET ALONG THE POTOMAC" • UP FROM SLAVERY •
TO THE PRESENT

3 GOVERNMENT AND ECONOMY   GOVERNING THE OLD DOMINION 48
INSIDE GOVERNMENT • "MOTHER OF PRESIDENTS" • SPEAKING OUT ABOUT
SCHOOLS • CONCERNED ABOUT CRIME • MORE JOBS AND BETTER PAY • COAL
AND ALTERNATE SOURCES OF ENERGY

4 PEOPLE   "PLAIN, HONEST . . . NEIGHBORS"   64
SCOTLAND IN VIRGINIA • RECIPE: CHOCOLATE CHESS PIE • RICHMOND'S JEWISH
HERITAGE • MANY VIRGINIAS

5 ACHIEVEMENTS   DYNAMIC PEOPLE   80
STRIDES IN BUSINESS AND INDUSTRY • WRITERS • MUSICIANS • ACTORS •
ATHLETES

6 LANDMARKS   EXPLORING VIRGINIA   96
THE EASTERN SHORE • THE TIDEWATER • THE PIEDMONT • THE MOUNTAIN
AND VALLEY REGION

STATE SURVEY   117
STATE IDENTIFICATIONS • SONG • GEOGRAPHY • TIMELINE • ECONOMY •
CALENDAR OF CELEBRATIONS • STATE STARS • TOUR THE STATE

FIND OUT MORE   139

INDEX   142

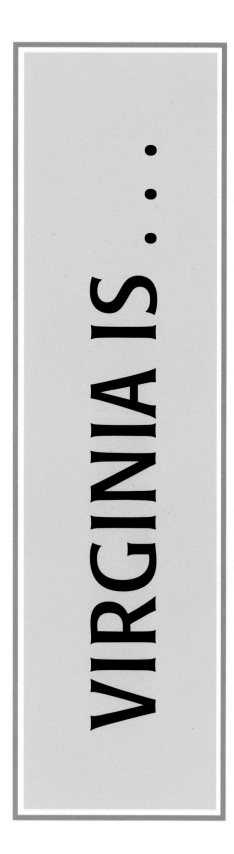

VIRGINIA IS . . . .

Virginia is beautiful land . . .

"Equal to the promised land in fertility, and far superior to it for beauty."
                                        —author Washington Irving

"Heaven and earth never agreed better to frame a place for man's habitation. Here are hills, plains, valleys, rivers and brooks, all running most pleasantly into a faire bay encompassed about with fruitful and delightsome land."   —Captain John Smith

. . . and proud people.

"I like your country, Virginia, and Virginians. Virginians are all snobs. I like snobs. A snob spends so much time being a snob he has none left to bother other people."
                              —author William Faulkner

"In Virginia, all the geese think they are swans."
                              —President John Adams

"If I lived away from my country a hundred years, I would still be a Virginian."
          —Nancy Astor, Viscountess Astor, Britain's American-born
                              first female member of Parliament

Virginians love politics . . .

"I am a Virginian, so naturally I am a politician."
                    —Nancy Astor, speech in England, 1919

. . . and above all, they love their state.

"You can work for Virginia, to build her up again, to make her great again. You can teach your children to love and cherish her."
                    —Confederate General Robert E. Lee to a young girl,
                              five years after the end of the Civil War.

"Good Old Dominion, the blessed mother of us all."
                                        —President Thomas Jefferson

"No one should ever ask a man whether he was born in Virginia because, if he was, he certainly will tell you himself, and if he was not, he will be ashamed to admit it."   —William Cabell Bruce

---

Virginia is history; the American Revolution started and ended there, and the Civil War was fought most bitterly within her borders. Virginia was the first of the thirteen colonies. The original Virginia Colony was carved up into many states (Kentucky, Ohio, Indiana, Illinois, Michigan, Wisconsin, Minnesota, and West Virginia), giving it the nickname "Mother of States." Eight presidents were born there, making it the "Mother of Presidents." King Charles I of England fondly called it his "Old Dominion," his much loved territory.

Virginia is government; most of the people who work for the federal government in Washington, D.C., live there. Virginia is beautiful beaches, rolling farmland, and mountains; small towns, busy cities, and quiet countryside. It is people with many kinds of jobs and many interests. Virginia is home to people of different races trying to live together, failing, and trying harder again.

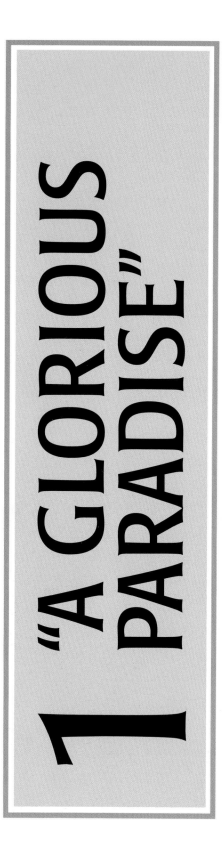

1 "A GLORIOUS PARADISE"

Three hundred million years ago, two flat pieces of the earth's surface, called tectonic plates, started to rub against each other under the vast sea that covered much of what is now Virginia. Although they moved incredibly slowly—just inches a year—they pressed against each other so hard and for so long that over the course of fifty million years they rose up from the ocean. The sea flowed off them, and their great ridges formed the Appalachian mountains. These mountains run down much of the east coast of the United States, including the western part of Virginia. Today, they are covered with plants and full of animals.

The lush fertility of Virginia is not new. Millions of years ago, it must have been one of the most lively spots on earth. Many dinosaur fossils have been found there. The coal deposits in the western part of the state are the fossilized remains of huge primordial forests. The limestone that runs under much of the dirt is made up of the fossilized bodies of the sea creatures that once lived in the primeval sea.

Later, when the first mammals roamed the earth, Virginia was the site of much life. Large numbers of mastodon fossils have been found there. In his *Notes on the State of Virginia* Thomas Jefferson says that Native American mythology identifies these fossils as the remains of monsters killed by Indian heroes.

In prehistoric times, the coast of what is now Virginia reached far

More deer roam Virginia today than before white people arrived on the American continent.

out into the Atlantic Ocean. But when the polar icecaps melted at the end of the Ice Age, the level of the ocean rose and flooded the land, moving the shoreline inland to about where it lies now. To this day, the eastern coast of the state is so low that much of it is marshland, which floods frequently.

Virginia is fairly small in size. It is the thirty-sixth largest state. Its shape reminds some people of an old-fashioned lady's slipper, with its toes pointing to the west and its heel on the bay. At the back of its top sits Washington, D.C. The state is bounded on the east by the Atlantic Ocean and the Chesapeake Bay, and shares its other borders with many states: Maryland (and Washington, D.C.) to the northeast, West Virginia to the west and northwest, Kentucky to the west, and Tennessee and North Carolina to the south.

MANY VIRGINIAS

Virginia can be divided into three main regions: the Tidewater on the east, the central Piedmont, and the western Mountain and Valley region. (Some people consider northern Virginia as a separate area, but we will include it here in the Tidewater.)

The Tidewater. Many rivers and creeks flow into the ocean in the eastern part of the state. They divide the land into long, narrow peninsulas, locally called "necks." The tidal flows of the ocean enter the wide mouths of many of the rivers, giving the region the nickname "Tidewater." The ocean water makes the river water brackish (salty and bad to drink) and has created many swamps. The largest is the 63,000-acre Great Dismal Swamp. To the early settlers, used to England's green fields and thick forests, this marsh with its snakes, mosquitoes, and unfamiliar creatures must have seemed gloomy. But to American-born George Washington, the Great Dismal Swamp was "a glorious paradise." His opinion is shared by many Virginians today.

The southern tip of the Eastern Shore is a flat, sandy, windswept area. This narrow strip of land hangs almost due south, cutting off the Chesapeake Bay from the ocean. It is also called the "Delmarva peninsula," a name made up of "DELaware," "MARy-

IN CELEBRATION OF BIRDS AND OYSTERS

The natural beauties of the Eastern Shore make it a good place to celebrate wildlife. Bird lovers flock to the two-day Eastern Shore Birding Festival each October to watch the migration of hundreds of songbirds, as well as the larger hawks and falcons. In November, parts of the wildlife refuge of Assateague Island that are usually off limits to humans are open to the public for Refuge Waterfowl Week. Here bird lovers get the chance to watch waterfowl migration at its peak.

The oysters that provide a livelihood for so many residents of the Eastern Shore are "thanked" in October. At that time Chincoteague Island hosts the Oyster Festival, where bands entertain people as they eat oysters and other kinds of local seafood.

land," and "VirginiA," the three states that share it. Many islands cluster around the peninsula.

The Piedmont. The Piedmont (French for "foothills") covers the central part of the state. Here the land starts to rise gently from the eastern lowlands on its way to the mountains farther west. The rolling land is fertile and covered with forests. Most of the trees here are the same kind that grew in that area centuries ago. There are few pines and many hardwoods, such as oak and maple.

The Piedmont is watered by many rivers, including the Potomac, the Rappahannock, the York, and the James. These rivers flow south-east to the Piedmont.

Mountain and Valley Region. The Appalachian Mountains rise out of the Piedmont foothills. The mountains are divided into different sections, of which the most important are the Alleghenies and the Blue Ridge Mountains, so called because the moist air rising out of them makes their ridges look blue-green. Lara Semones, who grew up in the Blue Ridge Mountains, says, "From any mountaintop, no matter what time of day, they have a blue hue to them." The western mountains hold the lovely Shenandoah Valley. The most important rivers of this area are the Shenandoah, the Clinch, and the New River.

A PLEASANT CLIMATE AND BEAUTIFUL BIRDS

Virginia has generally warm weather, although it tends to be cooler in the mountains than in the lower areas. Along the shore, temperatures of 50° F in midwinter are not uncommon, and the thermometer goes to well above 90° for much of the summer. Many people, both Virginians and visitors, take advantage of the hot and usually sunny summer weather to spend a lot of time at the beach. Norfolk's average temperature runs from 47° F in January to a high of 86° in July.

The area around Washington tends to be hotter and wetter. Gordon Duffus of Chester points out, "Our nation's capital was built in a swamp." The heat and humidity combine to make summers in northern Virginia steamy and uncomfortable.

Lara Semones says, "It's really nice to go into the Blue Ridge Mountains because you see so much beautiful farmland." This view of the Shenandoah Valley shows what she means.

In the mountains the weather is drier than in the Piedmont and especially in the Tidewater, where the warm ocean breezes bring high humidity ashore. The mountains also show the most spectacular fall foliage, attracting residents and tourists alike to view the trees as they turn color. Lara Semones says, "The climate is wonderful. We have four distinct seasons—the fall is yellow and red and orange. Lots of people like to ride their bikes along the Blue Ridge Parkway and just look at the colors. The winter, with the snow, is really gorgeous. You can see forever. There's dogwood everywhere in the spring. Summertime is hot and humid from July on. Everything is so green, and the farmland is just beautiful."

Rainfall is moderate throughout the state, as is snowfall. Even in the mountains, it is rare for more than two or three feet to fall in one winter.

People in Virginia take advantage of this pleasant climate: They swim in the ocean and the bay and hike, explore caves, and boat in the Piedmont and Mountain and Valley region. In the eighteenth century, Thomas Jefferson said, "We have reason to value highly the accident of birth in such a [climate] as that of Virginia." Modern Virginians agree with him.

Given Virginia's varied geography and mild climate, it is not surprising that many different kinds of animals and plants thrive in the state. More than half the state is covered with dense forest. Here deer and bear, as well as smaller mammals, find food and shelter.

The trees provide a home for many varieties of birds, ranging in size from the large wild turkeys to the brilliant red cardinals (the state bird). Many of these birds have feathers of spectacular

LAND AND WATER

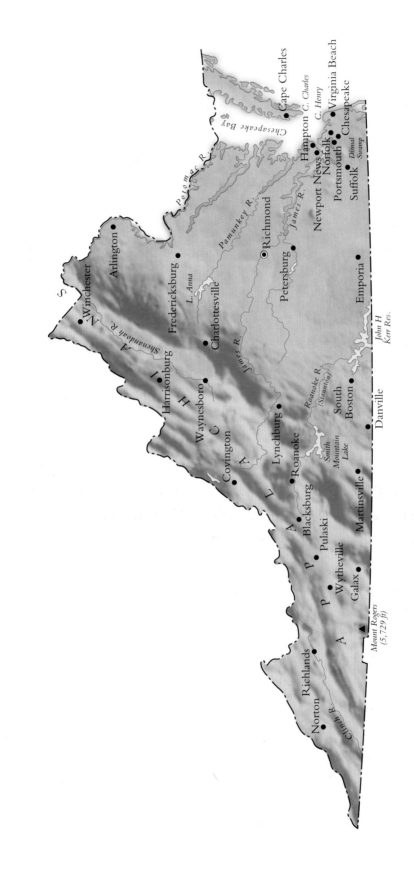

Cape Charles

C. Charles

C. Henry

Virginia Beach

Hampton

Chesapeake

Chesapeake Bay

Newport News

Norfolk

Portsmouth

Dismal Swamp

Suffolk

Potomac R.

Pamunkey R.

Richmond

James R.

Arlington

Fredericksburg

Petersburg

Winchester

L. Anna

Emporia

S

Charlottesville

John H Kerr Res.

N

Shenandoah R.

James R.

A

Harrisonburg

I

Roanoke R. (Staunton)

H

Waynesboro

South Boston

C

Danville

Covington

Lynchburg

Smith Mountain Lake

Martinsville

A

Roanoke

L

Blacksburg

A

Pulaski

P

Wytheville

P

Galax

A

Mount Rogers (5,729 ft)

Richlands

A

Norton

Clinch R.

Although beautiful, these Canadian geese can be a nuisance. They destroy people's gardens and honk loudly throughout the day.

colors, especially the orioles, scarlet tanagers, blue grosbeaks, and ruby-throated hummingbirds. They are very shy, and catching a glimpse of their brilliant plumage through the trees is a rare treat.

The Eastern Shore is also home to many birds—snow geese, herons, bald eagles, pelicans, falcons, and ducks—that depend on the sea for their food and are larger than the forest birds. Off the shore a lucky visitor can spot giant sea turtles, dolphins, and whales. Huge shad swim in the rivers and ocean.

"THE GREATEST PEOPLE IN THE WORLD"

Unitarian minister William Ellery Channing said in the 1830s that if the Virginians could only do without their slaves, he would "think them the greatest people in the world." Many people continue to feel this way and want to share in the greatness of the state. More and more people are moving there. The state's population rose by one million people between 1980 and 1990. The 1994 estimated census showed that about 6,552,000 people lived in Virginia, making it the twelfth most populated state in the country.

Historically, this is a decline. Virginia was the most populous colony, then the most populous state. By 1820, it had dropped to third place, and to seventh by 1860. Much of the drop is due to the fact that Virginia did not have many factories until this century. The immigrants that came to America in the nineteenth century were looking for industrial work. At that time, Virginia had few factories, so most of the European immigrants went up north instead.

Where people live has changed as well. In 1900, few Virginians lived in cities. Most were farmers or fishermen, who lived in small towns or in the country. But by 1955, more than half the population were city dwellers, and now nearly three-quarters of Virginians live in large cities, 10 percent in small cities, and only 20 percent in the country.

The growth in the state's population has not always been good for the environment. The Chesapeake Bay has long provided a livelihood for people who live by fishing, but recently the bay has become overfished. Sea life has deteriorated greatly in this century, due mostly to the pollution of the Chesapeake Bay.

Old meets new as this staff member of Colonial Williamsburg heads to work on her bike.

Forty-eight rivers empty into the bay. These rivers flow through heavily populated areas on their way to the bay, and carry with them industrial waste and fertilizer runoff from the farms. The fertilizer encourages the growth of algae to such an extent that the algae chokes off oxygen from the fish, causing them to die. Their rotting bodies further dirty the water. Few people even swim in the bay any more.

Cleanup efforts have begun but still have a long way to go. Virginians are aware that all creatures of the rivers, whether they live in the water or in the air above, depend upon a delicate balance. For their continuing survival, and that of the people who share their world, the waterways must be kept clean.

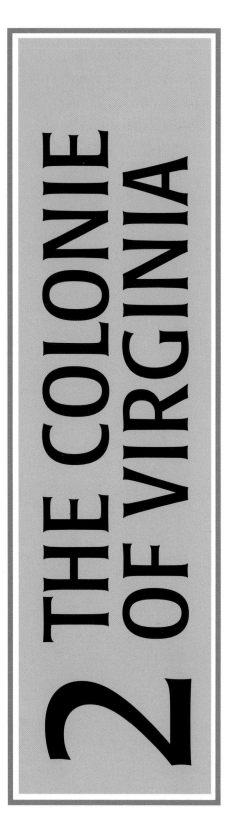

2 THE COLONIE OF VIRGINIA

Good Times in the New World (The Hope of Jamestown), by John Gadsby Chapman.

The first humans arrived in what is now Virginia between five and eight thousand years ago. They hunted, fished, gathered plants, and moved on. They began at some point to return to the same place year after year. They learned to burn the trees and brush in a small area, which left ashes on the ground. This ash changed the chemical makeup of the soil so that berries would grow better. When the people returned the next summer, they would have more berries to pick.

About two thousand years ago, some people began staying put long enough to grow corn. They cleared land near the sea, built houses, and hunted game. Several different tribes lived, for the most part peacefully, in different parts of the state. In the east were the Susquehanna and the largest group, the Powhatan. In the center were the Monacan and Manahoac, and in the west, the Cherokee.

Most of the tribes in what is now Virginia spoke the Algonquian language. Many of their villages were located near rivers, where the fishing was good. They usually lived in houses made of saplings lashed together and covered with bark. The speakers of Algonquian called the Eastern Shore "Accawmacke," and the early English mapmakers referred to Virginia as "the Colonie of Virginia and the Kingdom of Accawmacke."

These Virginian Indian chiefs are dressed more sensibly than the English settlers, who, wrote author Robert Beverley in 1705, "go sweltering [sweating] about in their thick Cloaths all the Summer, because they used to do so in their Northern climate; and then unfairly complain of the heat of the Country."

THE JAMESTOWN SETTLEMENT

Giovanni da Verrazano, an Italian who explored for the French government, was the first European to pass through Virginia, in about 1524. Fifty years later, Spanish priests opened a settlement on the York River. They didn't stay long.

The explorers liked what they saw, though. The woods were so thick that, as one historian has said, "in the seventeenth century,

GLOOSCAP AND THE BABY—
AN ALGONQUIAN TALE

Glooscap [both the first man and a god], having conquered the Kewawkqu', a race of giants and magicians, and the Medecolin, who were cunning sorcerers, and Pamola, a wicked spirit of the night, besides hosts of fiends, goblins, cannibals, and witches, felt himself great indeed, and boasted to a woman that there was nothing left for him to subdue.

But the woman laughed and said: "Are you quite sure, Master? There is still one who remains unconquered, and nothing can overcome him."

In some surprise Glooscap inquired the name of this mighty one.

"He is called Wasis," replied the woman, "but I strongly advise you to have no dealings with him."

Wasis was only a baby, who sat on the floor sucking a piece of maple sugar and crooning a little song to himself. Now Glooscap had never married and was ignorant of how children are managed, but with perfect confidence he smiled at the baby and asked it to come to him. The baby smiled back but never moved, whereupon Glooscap imitated a beautiful birdsong. Wasis, however, paid no attention and went on sucking his maple sugar. Unaccustomed to such treatment, Glooscap lashed himself into a rage and in terrible and threatening accents ordered Wasis to come to him at once. But Wasis burst into dire howls, which quite drowned the god's thundering, and would not budge for any threats.

Glooscap, thoroughly aroused, summoned all his magical resource. He recited the most terrible spells, the most dreadful incantations. He sang the songs which raise the dead, and those which send the devil scurrying to the nethermost depths. But Wasis merely smiled and looked a trifle bored.

At last Glooscap rushed from the hut in despair, while Wasis, sitting on the floor, cried, "Goo, goo!" And to this day the Indians say that when a baby says "Goo," he remembers the time when he conquered mighty Glooscap.

a squirrel could have crossed eastern North America from the Mississippi River to the Atlantic Ocean without touching the ground." There was abundant game, and the explorers had never before seen such enormous seafood—lobsters six feet long, for example. As Thomas Jefferson was to say more than a century later, "This scene is worth a voyage across the Atlantic."

An early English traveler was of the same opinion, writing to the king enthusiastically: "If Virginia had but horses and kine [cattle] in some reasonable proportion, I dare assure myself, being inhabited with English, no realm in Christendom were comparable to it."

In 1585 the English claimed a large area and named it Virginia in honor of Queen Elizabeth I, the "Virgin Queen." In 1606, King James I gave the land to the Virginia Company. The settlers were to explore, build a settlement, and convert the natives to Christianity. They landed at what is now Virginia Beach on April 26, 1607.

Their first impressions were very positive. One traveler wrote of "faire meddowes and goodly tall trees, with such Fresh Waters running through the woods as I was almost ravished at the first sight thereof." They built Jamestown, England's first permanent American town.

The settlers' first meeting with the native peoples seems to have terrified everyone. The settlers saw half-naked men "creeping upon all fours . . . like bears, with their bows in their mouths, [who] charged us very desperately in the faces." But when the settlers opened fire, the Indians, who had never heard gunshots before, ran in terror.

Despite its beauty, Jamestown turned out to be a terrible place for a town. The water was bad, and the land was swampy and filled with mosquitoes that carried disease. The colonists were mostly city people and didn't know how to farm, build houses, or hunt.

Two people helped the colonists survive. One was their leader, Captain John Smith, a short, very strong redhead only twenty-seven years old. He made maps of the region, adopting many of the Indian names, such as "Chesapeack," meaning "great shellfish bay." The other person was Pocahontas, the daughter of the Indian leader Powhatan. Smith described Powhatan as "a tall well proportioned man, with a sower [sour] look." Once Powhatan captured Smith. Smith probably made up the famous story that Pocahontas saved his life. But she did convince her father to be kind to the settlers several times.

John Smith was injured in a gunpowder explosion and had to return to England. Lacking leadership, the colony was in serious trouble. By the end of their first year, more than two-thirds of them had died. More settlers arrived in 1609, but the situation became even more grim. They had so little food in the winter of 1609–1610 that about 435 of the 500 residents died before spring. One survivor said: "Our men were destroyed with cruell diseases as Swellings, Fluxes, Burning Fevers . . . but for the most part they died of meere famine." This winter became known as the "starving time."

Even so, more colonists came in 1610. The Indians had taught them how to plant crops, but by then the English had realized how much money could be made by growing tobacco (which was unknown in Europe until this time). So instead of planting food,

Captain John Smith, who led the Jamestown settlers through their first tough winter.

they concentrated on tobacco. People became so crazy to make profits off this plant that they even planted seeds in the cracks of the streets! Not everyone approved of tobacco. King James called smoking a "custom loathsome to the eye, hateful to the nose, harmful to the brain, dangerous to the lungs."

A colonist named John Rolfe found a way to cure [dry] leaves for export to Europe. He married Pocahontas in 1614, after she was kidnapped by the English. Rolfe said that he married her not for "affection, but for the good of this plantation, for the honor of our country." She took the name "Rebecca Rolfe" and sailed to England

The marriage of Pocahontas to the English settler John Rolfe helped bring eight years of peace to the Virginia Colony.

Ætatis suæ 21 A°. 1616.

with him, dying there of a fever in 1617. Their son Thomas returned to Virginia, where he married and had children. Some Virginians today proudly claim Pocahontas as their ancestor.

THE WESTWARD PUSH

After Powhatan's death in 1618, a new chief led an attack on colonists, killing three hundred and fifty. In revenge, English troops forced the Indians out of the area into the west. By the 1650s, some colonists were also starting to move west into the Piedmont. The area was harder to farm, but there was a benefit: The abundant running water supplied power to mills, leading to the first factories in the area.

Communication between the settlers in the western part of Virginia and the colony's governing body, the House of Burgesses, was poor. These settlers became frustrated at their lack of power. In 1676, a group of western farmers led by Nathaniel Bacon rebelled against Governor Berkeley. They won more representation in the House of Burgesses. "Bacon's Rebellion" was the first American revolt against British authority.

After years of peaceful relations, Powhatans attacked the settlers, who in turn pushed the natives from their tribal lands.

By the eighteenth century, life had become more comfortable, at least for people with money. The wealthy sent their sons to the College of William and Mary in Williamsburg and often had tutors for their children. One tutor describes a typical morning in 1774: "Before Breakfast *Nancy & Fanny* had a Fight about a Shoe Brush which they both wanted—Fanny pull'd off her Shoe and threw it at Nancy, which missed her and broke a pane of glass of our School Room."

The French and Indian War, which lasted from 1754 to 1763, was a battle over land rights in the Americas. Many Virginians fought on the English side against the French and Indians over ownership of some of the colonies. One of these soldiers was young George Washington. He enjoyed military life, writing: "I heard the bullets whistle, and believe me, there is something charming in the sound." Washington served as an aide to British General Edward Braddock, who did not hold him in high regard. When rejecting some advice given to him by Washington, Braddock said haughtily, "These are high times when a British general is to take counsel of a Virginia buckskin."

The alliance with the British did not last long. The colonists were growing resentful of the way England controlled their lives. The Stamp Act, which forced the colonists to pay taxes on any official document, enraged them. When the king's governor closed the House of Burgesses in 1774, some Virginians and other colonists resolved to form a new country. "I am not a Virginian," said Patrick Henry, "but an American." One year later, Henry made a speech in Richmond, insisting, "Give me liberty, or give me death!"

Virginia's Thomas Jefferson wrote the Declaration of Indepen-

George Washington enjoyed being a soldier, but returned to his life as a farmer when his military and political careers were over.

Thomas Jefferson was a born revolutionary. In a letter to a friend, he wrote, "The tree of liberty must be refreshed from time to time with the blood of patriots and tyrants."

dence, which said the former colonies were now an independent country. England did not accept this statement, and war was declared. Although the words and actions of so many Virginians had led to this war, very little of it was actually fought on their land. Only the war's last battle and the final surrender of the British took place there, in Yorktown.

The new country needed laws. George Mason had written a large part of Virginia's constitution, and Thomas Jefferson relied heavily on this document to write the Constitution of the United States. Mason then wrote the Declaration of Rights, which would form the basis of the Bill of Rights, the first ten amendments to the Constitution.

"AN INHUMAN PRACTICE"

Virginia's first black people arrived in the colony in 1619, when twenty Africans from a Dutch slave ship were traded for food and water. They were indentured servants—once they had worked enough to pay for their passage, they would be free. The first slaves were brought to the colony in the 1640s.

In his *Notes on the State of Virginia,* Thomas Jefferson mentioned that an "inhuman practice once prevailed in this country, of making slaves of the Indians." Oddly, Jefferson did not seem to find the enslavement of Africans and American-born blacks inhuman. Although he said that he did not approve of owning slaves, he never freed his own.

Many farmers in Virginia used enslaved people to grow and harvest their crops. Over-planting of tobacco exhausted the soil, so the farmers needed more workers to make a profit. In the 1790s, Virginia had 270,000 slaves and 296,000 free citizens, both black and white. Virginia became an important center for buying and selling slaves. The lives of the slaves, never easy, got harder and harder.

A slave named Nat Turner thought that God wanted him to organize his fellow slaves to kill the white people. When a mysterious black spot moved across the face of the sun one day in August 1831, Nat said, "Just as the black spot passed over the sun, so shall the blacks pass over the earth." He led his followers through Southampton County, Virginia, killing dozens of white men, women, and children. The whites armed themselves and fought back, capturing Turner and killing hundreds of black people, most of whom had had nothing to do with the rebellion.

Slave traders often split up families as they moved their human cargo.

Turner was executed. His revolt had failed, but the white people, fearful of another attack, made life even more difficult for the slaves.

At the same time, the slave trade was growing in Virginia. In 1832, more than six thousand slaves were sold there. The tensions brought about by these sales, together with the new restrictions on blacks, sped up the beginning of the Civil War.

The issue of whether states could decide for themselves whether slavery was legal bitterly divided the nation. Finally, in 1861, eleven southern states seceded (removed themselves) from the Union, forming the Confederate States of America. The North and South were at war.

Unlike the Revolution, which had mostly bypassed Virginia, the Civil War raged in the state. Of the four thousand battles of the Civil War, two thousand two hundred were fought in Virginia. Many Virginians died. Before the disastrous battle of Gettysburg, General George Pickett encouraged his troops by saying, "Up, men, and to your posts! Don't forget today that you are from Old Virginia." The first sea battle between ironclad warships occurred at Hampton Roads, Virginia, in 1862, when the *Monitor* and the *Merrimack* (called the *Virginia* by the Confederates) fought a bloody fight.

During the Civil War, not only soldiers but also civilians suffered horribly. Richmond, the capital of the Confederacy, was the scene of bread riots in 1863. People desperate for food broke into stores and warehouses, taking everything edible they could lay their hands on. After four punishing years of the worst fighting Americans have ever known, the Confederate troops, under the

The historic sea battle between the Merrimac *and the* Monitor.

Virginian Robert E. Lee, surrendered at Appomattox Court House, Virginia.

People in Virginia are not likely to forget this war, even though it ended more than one hundred years ago. Every August, the Civil War Weekend is held in Manassas, Virginia, the site of the war's first major land battle. People dressed in Civil War costume lead tours, giving the history of the battle.

A reenactment of the Battle of Cedar Creek, in which Confederate troops were forced to retreat.

"A NOISE, TERRIFIC AS OF CRASHING WORLDS"

Cornelia Peake McDonald lived in Winchester, the scene of much bloody fighting during the Civil War. Her infant daughter died in August 1862 while battles raged around their home. She wrote the following description of what happened next.

After she was buried, I was lying in bed with a feeling only of indifference to everything, a perfect deadness of soul and spirit. If I had a wish it was the world, with its fearful trials and sorrows, its mockeries and its vanishing joys, could come to an end. Suddenly the house was shaken to its foundations, the glass was shivered from the windows and fell like rain all over me as I lay in bed; a noise, terrific as of crashing worlds, followed, prolonged for some fearful moments.

My first thought was that the world was really in its last convulsion. I could not move, but lay fixed and paralyzed. Then a cry, and my room door was burst open. "The town is on fire!" screamed Betty, rushing in. I got up and running across the hall to where the windows looked towards the town, and then saw the whole eastern sky lighted by the blaze of burning buildings, a long line of which was in one huge conflagration . . . . [The Union soldiers'] great magazine [gunpowder warehouse] had been blown up, which had caused the fearful noise . . . . A battle had take place a short distance off, and many killed on both sides. . . .

My boys in looking over the field for whatever they could find of arms or any thing else left behind in the haste of the fugitives, came across the mutilated remains of the poor creature who had been sent back to see if the fuse was burning. One foot was found in our garden.

ALL QUIET ALONG THE POTOMAC

Virginia saw its share of bloody battles during the Civil War—Bull Run and Richmond among them. But when no fighting broke out on any given day, a familiar War Department announcement published in the nation's newspapers was: "All quiet along the Potomac." One day in September 1861, these words followed the customary headline: "A picket [front-line guard] shot." In the November 30 edition of *Harper's Weekly,* under the title "The Picket Guard," this poem appeared. Within a short time the verses were set to music by various composers, both from the North and from the South.

Words by Mrs. Ethel Lynn Beers   Music by W. H. Godwin

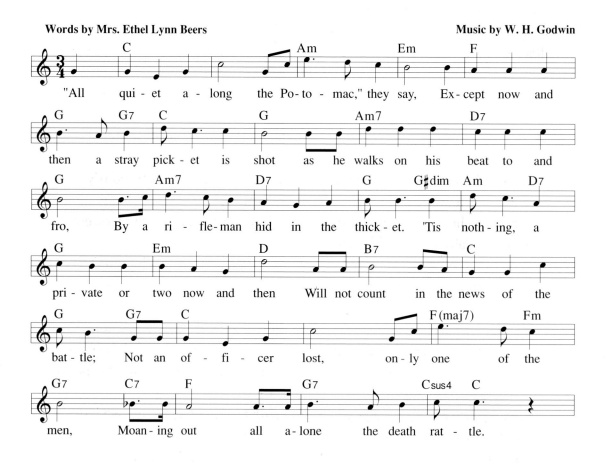

All quiet along the Potomac tonight,
Where the soldiers lie peacefully
   dreaming,
Their tents in the rays of the clear
   autumn moon,
O'er the light of the watch fires, are
   gleaming;
A tremulous sign, as the gentle night
   wind,
Through the forest leaves softly is
   creeping,
While stars up above, with their
   glittering eyes,
Keep guard for the army is sleeping.

There's only the sound of the lone
   sentry's tread,
As he tramps from the rock to the
   fountain,
And he thinks of the two in the low
   trundle bed,
Far away in the cot on the mountain.
His musket falls slack, and his face,
   dark and grim,
Grows gentle with memories tender,
As he mutters a prayer for the children
   asleep,
For their mother, may Heaven defend
   her.

The moon seems to shine just as
   brightly as then,
That night when the love yet unspoken

Leaped up to his lips when low-mur-
   mured vows
Were pledged to be ever unbroken.
Then drawing his sleeve roughly over
   his eyes,
He dashes off tears that are welling,
And gathers his gun closer up to its
   place
As if to keep down the heart-swelling.

He passes the fountain, the blasted
   pine tree,
The footstep is lagging and weary;
Yet onward he goes, through the broad
   belt of light,
Toward the shades of the forest so
   dreary.
Hark! Was it the night wind that
   rustled the leaves?
Was it moonlight so wondrously
   flashing?
It looks like a rifle—"Ah! Mary, good-
   bye!"
And the lifeblood is ebbing and
   splashing.

All quiet along the Potomac tonight,
No sound save the rush of the river;
While soft falls the dew on the face of
   the dead—
*[Skip to last beat of fourth from last
   measure]*
The picket's off duty forever.

UP FROM SLAVERY

Times were hard throughout the South in the years after the Civil War. During this period, known as Reconstruction, most of the former Confederate states, including Virginia, refused to accept the fourteenth amendment to the Constitution, which made slavery illegal. So the federal government put these states under military rule. Some Northerners, called "carpetbaggers" after their suitcases, made hastily from pieces of carpet, took terrible advantage of Southerners, both black and white. Virginia finally accepted the fourteenth amendment in 1870, and passed a state constitution acceptable to the federal government in Washington. Virginia was part of the Union again.

The end of slavery did not bring about equality between the races. In many cases, former slaves stayed on the plantations where they had been born and sharecropped (farmed the land, paying a share of the crop to its owner). Although they were legally free, the sharecroppers were as bound to the land and the white people as they had been under slavery.

Almost all the black population was uneducated, since strict laws had forbidden white people to teach them to read. Few were trained in useful skills. Some of the first reading lessons to former slaves and other blacks were given in Virginia under a tree later called the "Emancipation Oak." The nation's first mostly black university, Hampton University, was founded in Hampton, Virginia, in 1868. Booker T. Washington, a former slave and Hampton graduate, founded the Tuskegee Institute in Alabama. He wrote an autobiography, called *Up from Slavery,* to inspire other poor blacks to get an education and make a difference in their lives and in the world.

Despite these gains in education, the racial divide grew wider instead of more narrow. A new state constitution, adopted in 1902, took the right of voting away from black Virginians, and required the separation of the races in schools, transportation, and housing—in nearly every aspect of life. These regulations, which existed throughout the south, were called Jim Crow laws. Blacks suspected of small offenses, like being rude to a white person, were

In celebration of the Union victory ending slavery in the United States, some African Americans gave their children names like "Emancipation" and "Liberty." In truth, though, generations of blacks would have to struggle to gain equal treatment under the law.

lynched—attacked by a mob and killed, usually by hanging. Their bodies were sometimes left in public places to frighten other blacks. About one hundred blacks were lynched in Virginia between 1880 and 1920.

Most Virginians were horrified by lynching. They elected the dynamic Harry Flood Byrd to the governor's office in 1926, and in 1928 Byrd pushed through laws calling for swift and severe punishment for this crime.

TO THE PRESENT

More than one hundred thousand Virginians fought in World War I, many of them training at Virginia's Langley Air Force Base. World War II saw even more Virginians in uniform (three hundred thousand). Serving together in uniform led many Virginians to see that they were all the same and helped bring about the end of the cruel Jim Crow laws. Federal courts ordered schools desegregated in 1954. Many Virginians refused to obey this law at first. But finally, in 1959, public schools were integrated.

Many white people still resisted sending their children to schools with black children. In 1970, Virginia's Governor A. Linwood Holton showed his support for integration by personally taking his child to a black school in Richmond. Inspired by his example, other white people began to do the same. Lara Semones grew up in the town of Radford and attended the small high school there. She says, "I went to a high school that was almost exactly half black and half white, and the first time I noticed racial tensions was after I left there. We got along quite well." She recalls with pride her small

POPULATION GROWTH: 1790–1990

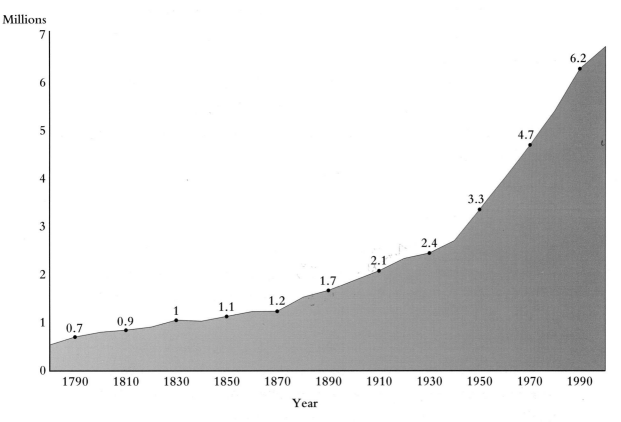

Millions

town's valiant efforts to keep members of the racist organization the Ku Klux Klan from marching through Radford.

The people who overcame the "starving time," the Revolution, the Civil War, and Reconstruction are working to defeat this enemy, racism, as well.

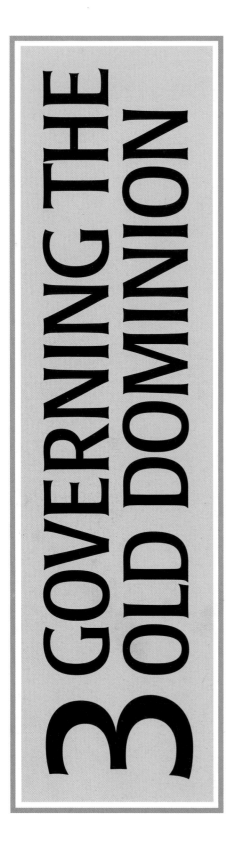

3 GOVERNING THE OLD DOMINION

Virginia's Capitol, completed in 1785, was designed by Thomas Jefferson.

The part of Virginia closest to Washington, D.C., is home to 1,864,000 people. About 500,000 of them work for the United States government. You might think that with so many Virginians spending all day working for the federal government, they would have little interest in the running of their own state. But this is not the case. Virginians are constantly changing laws and making new ones. As recently as 1970, Virginia adopted a totally new state constitution.

Virginia sends ten representatives and two senators to the United States Congress. They are nearly evenly divided between the two major parties. In 1995 six representatives were Democrats and four were Republicans. One senator was Republican, and one Democrat.

INSIDE GOVERNMENT

Like the United States and most states, Virginia has three branches of government: the legislative, the executive, and the judicial.

Legislative. In 1619, the citizens of Virginia formed a legislative body that they called the House of Burgesses. The present-day State Assembly is the direct descendant of the House of Burgesses, making it the oldest group of elected officials in the United States.

The State Assembly is divided into two houses, the Senate (with

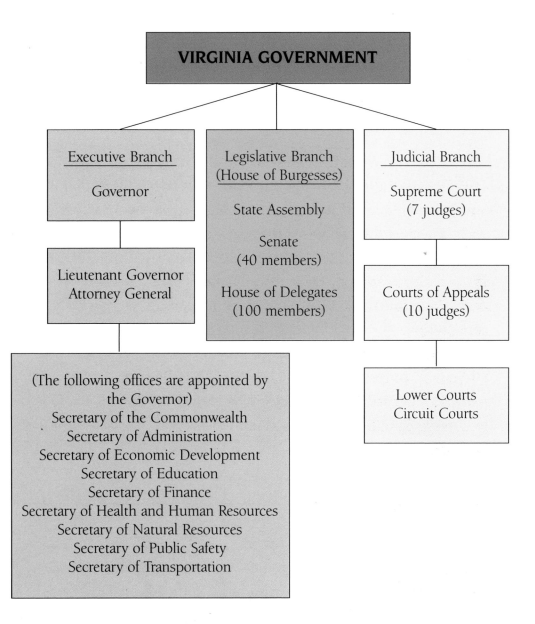

VIRGINIA GOVERNMENT

Executive Branch

Governor

Lieutenant Governor
Attorney General

(The following offices are appointed by
the Governor)
Secretary of the Commonwealth
Secretary of Administration
Secretary of Economic Development
Secretary of Education
Secretary of Finance
Secretary of Health and Human Resources
Secretary of Natural Resources
Secretary of Public Safety
Secretary of Transportation

Legislative Branch
(House of Burgesses)

State Assembly

Senate
(40 members)

House of Delegates
(100 members)

Judicial Branch

Supreme Court
(7 judges)

Courts of Appeals
(10 judges)

Lower Courts
Circuit Courts

forty members serving four-year terms) and the House of Delegates
(one hundred members serving two-year terms). The leader of each
house is elected by the other members. The assembly makes the

state laws, decides on the amount of taxes, and approves how state money is to be spent. Since the state has so many expenses, the legislature decided to earn some more money through a lottery. It has been very successful. Virginia earned $378 million from the lottery in 1993.

Executive. This branch consists of three elected officials and a number of appointed officials. The governor, the lieutenant governor, and the attorney general are elected.

The governor's most important jobs are to enforce the laws and to prepare the state's budget (spending plan). Like some other states, Virginia has a law that says the state must have a balanced budget, spending no more money in any year than it takes in through taxes and the lottery.

The governor may veto (cancel) any laws passed by the assembly, although if two-thirds of the members of the assembly vote against the veto, the veto is itself cancelled. The governor is also the commander-in-chief of the state police and the Virginia militia. Governors serve for four years in each term and may not have two terms in a row.

The lieutenant governor helps the governor and also takes over the governor's job if the governor dies or becomes too sick to govern. The attorney general is the chief legal advisor to the governor and often works with members of the judicial branch.

Judicial. This branch is made up of the court system. The courts interpret the laws written by the assembly and try legal cases. The most important court, the state supreme court, consists of seven justices, whose leader is called the chief justice. They serve twelve-year terms. Lower courts include the court of appeals, thirty-one circuit courts, district courts, and many juvenile and domestic-relations courts.

"MOTHER OF PRESIDENTS"

Eight American presidents were born in Virginia, more than in any other state. This includes four of the first five: George Washington (president 1789–1797), Thomas Jefferson (1801–1809), James Madison (1809–1817), James Monroe (1817–1825). The other four were William Henry Harrison (1841, died in office), John Tyler (1841–1845), Zachary Taylor (1849–1850, died in office), and Woodrow Wilson (1913–1921).

Not only presidents, but other national politicians have come from Virginia. Patrick Henry (1736–1799), the patriot whose brilliant speeches put into words what so many colonists were thinking about independence from England, was a member of the House of Burgesses. He also served a term as Virginia's governor.

Many members of the First Continental Congress, whose members decided that the colonies had to become free of England, were Virginians. Among them was the Continental Congress's first president, Peyton Randolph (1721–1775).

John Marshall (1755–1835) started his career in local Virginia politics, and became chief justice of the United States in 1801. Marshall is the person responsible for the fact that the Supreme Court is a strong branch of government.

In more recent times, George Catlett Marshall (1880–1959) served as the chief of staff of the United States Army, secretary of state, and secretary of defense. He is most famous as the author of

Patrick Henry is giving his powerful speech, which helped galvanize the colonists to rebel against British rule.

the European Recovery Plan, usually known as the Marshall Plan. This plan was used to rebuild Europe after World War II and won him the Nobel Peace Prize in 1953.

L. Douglas Wilder was elected governor of Virginia in 1989. The grandson of a slave, Wilder achieved many firsts: the first black in the Virginia senate since Reconstruction, the first black lieutenant governor of Virginia, and the first black governor of any state in America.

Virginia's John W. Warner served as secretary of the Navy from 1972 to 1974 and has been a U.S. Senator since 1979.

SPEAKING OUT ABOUT SCHOOLS

In most school districts, a school board makes decisions about which textbooks will be used, who will be the principals, what days school will be in session, and other matters. Until recently, Virginia was the only state in the United States in which the members of the school board were appointed by judges or other officials. Finally the Virginians passed a law saying that the people who live in the school district should elect the school board members. Ethel-Marie Underhill, who lives near Roanoke, thinks that this will make a big difference in education. She says, "I'm pleased that school

L. Douglas Wilder had long been active in civil rights when he was sworn in as Virginia's governor in 1990. His children look on at the ceremony on a cold January day in Richmond.

boards are now elected in Virginia, like all other states. It's nice to have public input."

Kapanga Kasongo, originally from Zaire, and now a professor at the University of Richmond, lives near Richmond. He says that the schools in the city don't have as much money to spend on education as the schools in the nearby counties. He says that the county schools "are among the best in the country." He adds, "A lot of people are moving away from the city of Richmond, and more and more people are moving ten, twenty, thirty miles from the city. It puts enormous financial pressure on the city. Comes the

A teacher helps children work at computers.

morning everybody flocks to Richmond, but they don't pay taxes there."

The schools are supported by local taxes, so if people who work in Richmond don't live there, they don't pay as many taxes to Richmond as city residents do. Meanwhile, they are using the city's resources, like the streets, the sewers, the libraries, and the museums. This means that the schools in the city have less money to spend than the county schools.

CONCERNED ABOUT CRIME

Virginia deals harshly with criminals. It has the death penalty and executed fourteen convicted felons between 1990 and 1993. This is more than any other state except Texas.

Children too can suffer severe criminal punishments in Virginia. Some legislators are concerned with the number of crimes committed by young people. In 1996, the assembly passed reforms to the juvenile justice system. Under these reforms, anyone aged fourteen or over who is charged with a serious crime, such as murder or rape, must be punished as an adult. If convicted, the child receives the same punishment as an adult who committed the crime and goes to an adult jail. The new law also makes it easier for school systems to send disruptive children to an alternative school. It also says that children must be tested for emotional problems when they are very young, so they can start being treated sooner. Virginia's Attorney General Jim Gilmore calls this a "balanced package" of laws.

Some people say this law could actually increase the amount of juvenile crime. Many young people, particularly those in gangs, are proud of going to jail. The threat of a long jail term may not prevent some of them from committing a crime. Attorney General Gilmore argues that unless something is done to slow down the number of crimes committed by young people, Virginia will see "more rape victims, more murder victims, more funerals, more graves. The time has come to prevent them from hurting other people." Time will tell which opinion is right.

The different regions of Virginia have varying rates of crime. For example, although the state as a whole has a low crime rate, Richmond usually ranks third or fourth in murder of all cities in the nation. The city is working to reduce its murder rate. The counties have lent police officers to Richmond, and the new police chief is trying community policing. Police cover smaller beats, so they have time to get to know residents and hopefully build good relationships with them.

MORE JOBS AND BETTER PAY

The end of slavery also brought an end to the era when Virginia was dependant upon trade in tobacco and human beings for its economic well-being.

Tobacco farming is a source of argument in the state. Each year, Virginia makes almost $200 million from its sale. Farmers earn thirty-eight times as much money per acre from tobacco as from wheat. So when the federal government proposes to raise the sales tax on cigarettes, Virginia's tobacco farmers try to convince their congressional representatives to oppose this increase. Tobacco is still an important crop.

The workers in Virginia are less dependent upon tobacco than they were in the colonial era, though. Today, manufacturing, especially of chemicals, processed foods, cloth, yarn, paper, plastics, and—still—cigarettes provides most jobs for Virginians.

During the two world wars, more manufacturing moved to Virginia as large shipyards located there to make ships for the war effort. Today, the Newport News Shipbuilding and Dry Dock

King James I of England was astonished "that the sweetness of man's breath . . . should be wilfully corrupted by this stinking smoke." Yet, the tobacco planted by his colonists remains a major crop in Virginia today.

Company is the largest privately owned shipyard in the world. Huge ships pull into the docks for repairs, and new ships are built and launched there.

Furniture and clothing factories also have operations in the state. More recently, high-tech silicon-producing industries have moved there. Northern Virginia has more than one thousand computer communication companies. Today, about 450,000 Virginians work in manufacturing.

The great numbers of people who live in northern Virginia are always needing new homes, schools, and stores. This busy building activity accounts in part for the size of the state's construction industry, which employs roughly 200,000 Virginians.

Farming is still an important industry. The fertile plains of the state yield the most crops in Virginia. Most of the state's 50,000 farmers live and work there. They provide dairy products, cattle, tobacco, chickens and turkeys, corn, hay, peanuts, apples, cucumbers, and soybeans.

1995 GROSS STATE PRODUCT: $154 BILLION

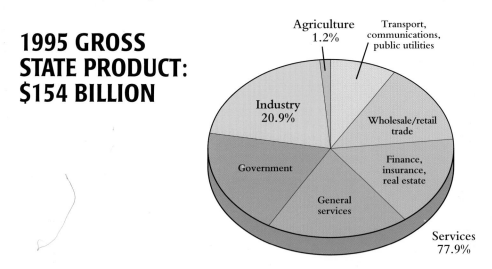

Agriculture 1.2%

Transport, communications, public utilities

Industry 20.9%

Wholesale/retail trade

Government

Finance, insurance, real estate

General services

Services 77.9%

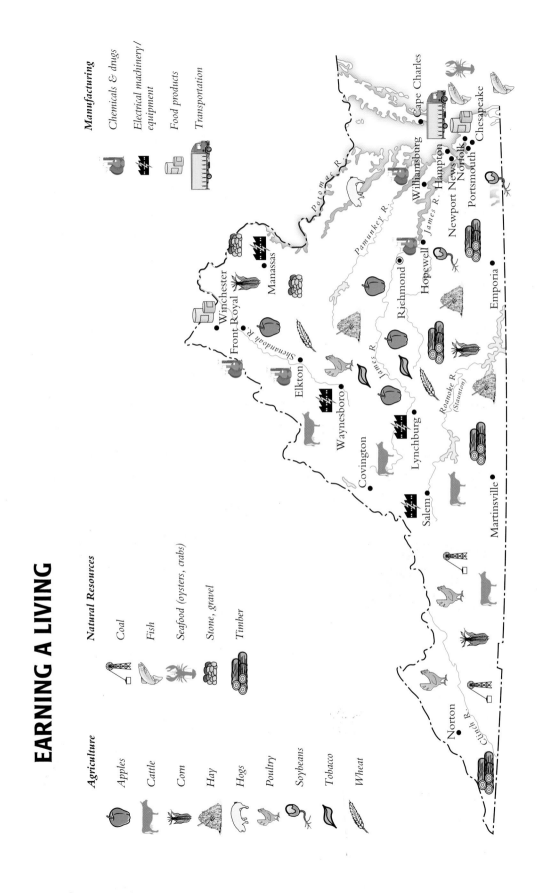

EARNING A LIVING

Agriculture

Apples

Cattle

Corn

Hay

Hogs

Poultry

Soybeans

Tobacco

Wheat

Natural Resources

Coal

Fish

Seafood (oysters, crabs)

Stone, gravel

Timber

Manufacturing

Chemicals & drugs

Electrical machinery/ equipment

Food products

Transportation

Virginian's average pay in 1993 was $25,496, slightly higher than the national average. The number of people living in poverty in Virginia fell from 12 percent to 10 percent between 1980 and 1993. This was much better than the rest of the country. At the same time that the number of poor Virginians fell, the number of poor Americans actually rose—from 13 percent to 15 percent. The percent of Virginia workers who are unemployed is also smaller than in the country as a whole. Virginia's economy has obviously boomed.

As a means of making a living, fishing is on the decline in Virginia. This oysterman's children will probably not "follow the water" when they choose a profession.

Not all workers share in this prosperity. For example, fishing has always employed many people in the state. But the increase in manufacturing, while it has given jobs to many Virginians, has caused pollution in the bay and along the ocean coast. This pollution has killed many shellfish in the water, forcing many people whose families had fished for generations to look for other jobs.

Tourists spend a lot of money in Virginia. In 1993, tourists spent more than $9 *billion* in the state. Many Virginians have jobs in tourism, introducing travelers to the wonders of their state.

COAL AND ALTERNATE SOURCES OF ENERGY

In 1970, Virginia produced 35 million tons of coal. A few years later, a world wide oil shortage forced Americans to turn to other sources of energy. Suddenly the coal fields in Virginia became more important. Mining, always an industry that had provided work for some Virginians, became a larger employer. Coal production climbed steadily to a peak of 47 million tons in 1990. Since then, the oil situation has eased and many scientists are searching for other forms of energy (solar, wind, etc.), so the coal-mining business is once again experiencing a slowdown. Production in 1993 dropped to 39 million tons.

The people of Virginia have had to change their way of earning a living many times. As the new century nears, the world's use of fossil fuels will have to drop even further as supplies run out. Virginians, used to adapting to change, will probably make good use of the manufacturing and technology industries already in place in their state.

4 "PLAIN, HONEST NEIGHBORS"

Thomas Jefferson wrote of Virginia, "This country . . . consists of plain, honest, and rational neighbors, . . . hospitable and friendly." Not everyone would agree with him. The Native Americans, for example, whose lands were taken from them, might disagree. Indians used to be free to live and hunt throughout the entire state of Virginia. Now, only tiny parts of the state remain in their control: the Pamunkeys, once the largest group of the Powhatan Confederacy, live on a small 800-acre reservation; the Mattaponis survive on merely 125 acres.

As long ago as 1609, some white people objected to the theft of these lands. In that year, Reverend Robert Gray asked his congregation, "By what right or warrant can we enter into the land of these Savages, take away their rightfull inheritance from them, and plant ourselves in their places, being unwronged or unprovoked by them?" But few shared his point of view, and the white people continued to push the Native Americans off their land. Today, less than 1 percent of the state's population claims Indian ancestry.

Relations between blacks and whites have not been much more pleasant. Although Jim Crow laws and the era of lynching are in the past, racial division is still strong. Most children attend schools made up almost entirely of children of their own race.

The people of Virginia are trying to help the races get along better. Each January, Lee-Jackson-King day honors Robert E. Lee, "Stonewall" Jackson, and Martin Luther King, Jr., all of whom were born in January. Lee and Jackson, the two most famous Confederate Army generals, were from Virginia and their statues stand on Richmond's Monument Avenue. The celebration of their birthdays caused anger in the black community, so Dr. King's was added to honor a black hero, too.

Susan McArthur moved to the rural part of the Piedmont in 1967. She says that in the country, unlike the cities, there is a strict

At age eighty-one, this man has seen many changes in race relations in his native Virginia.

division between the races. She points out, "The underclass is black and, because it's rural and agricultural, they're very poor and relatively uneducated. We don't have a middle-class black population in the farming areas."

The whites in Virginia come from many different lands. The early non-Indian population of Virginia was mostly English, with some Irish, Scottish, Welsh, French, and German as well. This mix has changed through the centuries. Today, three-quarters of the state's population is of European heritage, with ancestors mostly from Britain and Germany. A little more than one-fifth of the Virginians are black, and this proportion is expected to rise. About 220,000 are Asian and 193,000 are Hispanic. American Indians number about 15,000, or less than 1 percent of the population.

Some of these ethnic groups enjoy special festivals. The capital city of Richmond hosts many ethnic fairs. Kapanga Kasongo

ETHNIC VIRGINIA

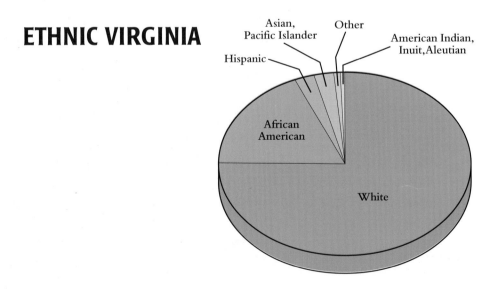

particularly enjoys October, when different groups are honored. In that month Richmond hosts an African fair, a Columbus Day festival when Italians take center stage, and Oktoberfest, celebrating Germany. "There's always something going on," Kasongo says.

SCOTLAND IN VIRGINIA

The first Scots came to Virginia as indentured servants. More Scots came in the eighteenth century, when many of them unsuc-

A Scottish-American boy sports a traditional kilt.

CHOCOLATE CHESS PIE

No one knows for sure where the name "chess pie" comes from. One explanation is that it doesn't have any special ingredients, so it's not apple pie, peach pie, or pumpkin pie—it's "jes' pie." Whatever the origin of the name, chess pie is a southern favorite, and this variation with chocolate won the blue ribbon at the Virginia State Fair for Pat Heath, of New Kent, Virginia.

Yield: 6 to 8 servings
2 cups sugar
2 Tablespoons cornstarch
4 eggs
1 can (8 oz.) chocolate-flavored syrup
1/4 cup milk
1/4 cup butter, melted
1 unbaked pie shell

Ask an adult to help you combine the sugar, cornstarch, eggs, chocolate-flavored syrup, milk, and butter in a bowl. Beat until smooth, using an electric mixer at medium speed. Pour into an unbaked pie shell. Bake in 350-degree oven 55 minutes or until center is set. Cool on rack.

cessfully supported their King James's claim to the throne of England. Some of the rebels who were caught were sent as prisoners to the penal colony of Carolina and Virginia. Still others were sent to the colonies to ease overcrowding at home. Most of them were bankers, tradesmen, and merchants involved in the import/export trade.

Alexandria was founded as a trading post by Scots. Dumfries, Fredericksburg, and Petersburg all had many Scots as their founding fathers and mothers. The Shenandoah Valley was originally opened up and farmed by Scotch-Irish and German immigrants.

Many of today's Virginians enjoy celebrating their Scottish past. Virginia is home to the second largest Scottish festival in the United States, the Scottish Games and Gathering of the Clans, held every July in Alexandria. As many as 200,000 people attend this festival each year, many of them wearing traditional Scottish clothes. They eat Scottish food, play traditional Scottish games, compete in country dancing, and enjoy the music of the bagpipes.

RICHMOND'S JEWISH HERITAGE

The city of Richmond is home to the sixth oldest synagogue in the United States. In the eighteenth century, the small city of Richmond had twenty-five hundred free people—slaves were not counted—including a Jewish population of one hundred. This was a larger percentage than either New York or Philadelphia had at that time.

The Jewish cemetery of Beth Shalome was inaugurated in 1791. Its founders underestimated the size of the population that would use it, and by 1816 it was already full and a new "Hebrew Cemetery" was opened nearby.

For the most part, the Jewish population in Richmond led lives quite similar to their non-Jewish neighbors. They owned slaves,

Jewish residents in nineteenth-century Richmond.

although some objected to the practice. They participated in the economic fortunes of the city. Their young men went off to fight in the Confederate Army, and those who were killed were buried in the world's only Jewish military cemetery outside of Israel.

Today, Church Hill is the home of Kenesseth Israel synagogue, founded in 1856. A large percentage of the city's Jewish population still lives in that neighborhood, where their ancestors lived and worshiped before them.

Richmond's Beth Ahabah Museum and Archives, containing papers and other materials telling about the lives of the Jewish community in Richmond, is open to the public.

MANY VIRGINIAS ·

Even though more people have jobs in Virginia than in most of the rest of the United States, this is not equally true throughout the state. The coal country of the west is concerned with the decline in the coal industry. Many northern Virginians have lost their jobs as the federal government gets smaller. And the fishermen along the bay are concerned about the declining sizes of their catches.

Farmers in rural Scott County continue to face hard times.

DRY FRYE: A VIRGINIA FOLKTALE

One time there was an old man named Dry Frye. . . . And one time he stayed for supper and he was eatin' fried chicken so fast he got a chicken bone stuck in his throat. Choked him to death. Well, the man of the house he was scared. "Law me!" he says, "they'll find old Dry Frye here and they'll hang me for murder sure!" So he took old Dry Frye to a house down the road a piece and propped him up against the door. Somebody went to go out the door and directly old Dry Frye fell in the house. "Law me!" says the man of the house. "Hit's old Dry Frye!" (Everybody knew old Dry Frye.) "We got to get shet of him quick or we're liable to be hung for murder!"

So he took old Dry Frye and propped him up in the bresh 'side the road. And way up in the night some men come along, thought it was a highway robber layin' for 'em. So they chunked rocks at him, knocked him down, and when they seen who it was (everybody knew old Dry Frye) they thought they'd killed him, and they got scared they'd be hung for murder. . . .

Well, they took old Dry Frye and propped him up against a man's cornhouse. And that man he went out early the next mornin'; and he's been missin' corn—so when he seen there was somebody over there at his cornhouse he ran and got his gun. Slipped around, hollered, "Get away from there or I'll shoot!"

The people of western Virginia have traditionally been an independent group. The west has felt isolated since the days when Nathaniel Bacon led his rebellion in 1676 against the House of Burgesses. An early settler in the west, Adam O'Brien, said he hated "those varmints, the sheriffs and constables." He said that earlier

And when old Dry Frye never moved he shot and Dry Frye tumbled over and hit the ground.

"Law me!" says the man. "I believe that was old Dry Frye." (Everybody knew Dry Frye.) "Now I've done killed him and I'll sure get hung for murder."

[Dry Frye has more misadventures, until he is found by an old woman and her family.]

Well, they had some wild horses in a wilderness out on the mountain. So they rounded up one of 'em, put him in the barn. Then they put an old no-'count saddle on him and an old piece of bridle, and put old Dry Frye on . . . and opened . . . the barn door and let the horse go. He shot out of there and down the road he went with that old preacher-man a-bouncin' first one side and then the other. And them rogues run out and went to shootin' and hollerin', "He's stole our horse! Stop him! Somebody stop him yonder! Horse thief! Horse thief!"

Everybody down the road come runnin' out their houses a-shoutin' and hollerin' and a-shootin' around, but that horse had done jumped the fence and took out up the mountain and it looked like he was headed for Kentucky.

And as far as I know old Dry Frye is over there yet a-tearin' around through the wilderness on that wild horse.

settlers had "lived quite happy before the Revolution, for then there was no law, no courts and no sheriffs [but] then came the lawyers and next the preachers, and from that time they never had any peace anymore."

In the Piedmont, country life resembles life in nineteenth-century England, says Susan McArthur. The wealthier people live in beautiful old houses, and have servants. Many of them send their children to boarding schools. She says, "In other parts of the country, people judge you by your education, your job, even your income. Here, the important thing to find out is 'What's your family name? How long have you been here?'" Even the countryside looks like England.

Politically, the citizens of the Tidewater and Piedmont areas are more liberal than those of the west. It has been said that the Appalachians form a "great spine of Republicanism which runs down the back of the [mostly Democratic] South."

In this century, many of the barriers between the east and the west have been lowered. Differences still exist, however. Ethel-Marie Underhill lives near Roanoke, in southwestern Virginia. She says, "I moved here from Kansas and found it harder to get acquainted with local people since they're more reserved than midwesterners." Susan McArthur shares her opinion, saying, "After thirty years, I still feel like an outsider because I wasn't born here."

Lara Semones agrees, but adds, "On the other hand, you have a community that really cares about each other and wants to help each other. People help out when there's a death in the family or illness."

Northern Virginians sometimes feel even more isolated. Most of that part of the state is filled with suburbs of Washington, D.C., and the residents have more in common with the northern United States than with the rest of their state. Sally Goldfarb of Winchester says, "I never felt southern." But her husband decided to prove to her that Virginia is part of the south. He showed her the confeder-

"It's a gracious way of life. When I first visited this area I thought I had stepped into nineteenth-century England," says Susan McArthur.

ate flag in Winchester's town square. Finally, a visit to Winchester's Confederate graveyard was enough to convince her that the city was indeed a southern town.

Lara Semones, on the other hand, is from the southern part of Virginia and has always felt like a real southerner. She is upset by the prejudices many people in other parts of the United States have against southerners and says, "When I moved up north I was labeled as being unintelligent, super-conservative, and racist because I was from the south. I felt like an ambassador and was constantly defending the south."

In the end, Virginia stands for many things, and throughout its history it has drawn people from different races and faiths to settle in and call it home.

A veteran of World War I pays his respects at Arlington National Cemetery.

5 DYNAMIC PEOPLE

Virginia has many well-known politicians, but it is also proud of its residents who have stood out in such areas as business, the arts, and sports.

STRIDES IN BUSINESS AND INDUSTRY

Manufacturing and business came late to Virginia. Still, some Virginians have made important contributions in these fields. Cyrus McCormick was an early inventor, and he combined his knowledge of farming with his genius for invention and salesmanship to become an early American success story.

Born in 1809 in Rockbridge County, Virginia, Cyrus McCormick was a farm boy who saw how difficult it was to harvest wheat. His desire to make this job easier led to his invention of the reaper, which made the job much easier. He was one of the first manufacturers to standardize parts, so if a piece of a reaper broke a farmer could buy a replacement piece and be confident that it would fit his machine exactly.

McCormick was also a pioneer in the field of credit. Farmers could pay a small part of the price of the reaper, take it home, and use it, all the while making payments until they had paid the entire cost of the machine. McCormick's factories made more than six million reapers before his death in 1884. The McCormick reaper

Cyrus McCormick's first reaper was tested at Steele's Tavern, Virginia, in 1831. Painting by N. C. Wyeth.

is largely responsible for the great migration of Americans to the plains of the midwest. After his death, McCormick's company merged with several others to form the International Harvester Company, which still produces farm machinery today.

Another Virginian well-known in business also came from a family that was not originally in business. Born in Richmond in

1867, just two years after the end of the Civil War, Maggie Walker was the daughter of slaves. Maggie helped her mother, a laundress, scrub clothes before school. She had to get up at dawn to build a fire to heat the water, fill the tubs, and scrub clothes with harsh soap that left her hands raw and sore. Even with all this hard work, she graduated at the top of her class. When she and her classmates learned that they would not be allowed to graduate in the same building as the white students, they went on strike. This is the first known strike of black students in America.

Maggie Walker joined a society to aid the sick when she was fourteen years old. In 1903 she helped set up a bank aimed at black customers. This bank became so successful that it loaned the city of Richmond $100,000 to keep schools open at a time when none of the white banks could afford to help.

Walker was the first woman in the United States to found a bank and serve as its president, using her intelligence and talents to succeed in the largely white male world of business. Eleanor Roosevelt, wife of President Franklin D. Roosevelt, wrote to her, "I cannot imagine anything more satisfying than a life of the kind of accomplishments you have had." When she died in 1934, the *Richmond Times-Dispatch* said, "Her death leaves a gap in the ranks of American leadership. . . . There is no one at the moment who can replace her." Her Richmond home has been restored to its 1930s appearance and is open to tourists.

WRITERS

Virginians have always been writers. One of the best known is Edgar Allan Poe. This author of horror stories was born in Boston

Despite Edgar Allan Poe's serious expression and his terrifying stories and poems, he loved playing with the children in his Richmond neighborhood.

but was raised and educated in Richmond after his parents died when he was two years old. Although he lived in many states during his short life—he died at age forty—he considered Virginia his home.

Poe attended Jefferson University (now the University of Virginia) in Charlottesville. It was there he began the drinking and gambling that were to shorten his life. He married thirteen-year-old Virginia Clemm in 1836. Despite the difference in their ages, the marriage seemed happy, until Virginia died in 1847 of tuberculosis, the same disease that had killed Poe's parents. Poe wrote his most tragic poems and stories after her death. He spent the rest of his life in Richmond and died under mysterious circumstances in Baltimore.

Ellen Bryant Voigt was born and raised in Virginia and now lives in Vermont. In this poem, she talks about the hard existence of the country woman who imagines flying above all the work and difficulty of her life.

Farm Wife

Dark as the spring river, the earth
opens each damp row as the farmer
swings the far side of the field.
The blackbirds flash their red
wing patches and wheel in his wake,
down to the black dirt; the windmill
grinds in its chain rig and tower.

In the kitchen, his wife is baking.
She stands in the door in her long white
gloves of flour. She cocks her head and
tries to remember, turns like the moon
toward the sea-black field. Her belly
is rising, her apron fills like a sail.
She is gliding now, the windmill churns
beneath her, she passes the farmer,
the fine map of the furrows.
The neighbors point to the bone-white
spot in the sky.

Let her float
like a fat gull that swoops and circles,
before her husband comes in for supper,
before her children grow up and leave her,
before the pulley cranks her down
the dark shaft, and the church blesses
her stone bed, and the earth seals
its black mouth like a scar.

Virginian Earl Hamner Jr. is a much different kind of writer from Poe. He drew on his love for his native Virginia, where he was born in 1923, as inspiration for his film, "Spencer's Mountain." The saga of this poor and loving family is based on Hamner's own boyhood in the Appalachians. The film was turned into the long-running television series, "The Waltons." Hamner received an Emmy award for a Walton Christmas special called "The Homecoming." He also created the very different but equally popular television series "Falcon Crest."

Like Hamner, author William Styron never forgot his roots in Virginia. He was born in Newport News and left his native state for New York, where he first worked as an editor. He was not happy at this job, however, and turned to his main love—writing. Although Styron has lived in North Carolina, New York, Paris, and Connecticut, he uses Virginia for the settings of most of his work.

Styron is most famous for his novel *The Confessions of Nat Turner,* a fictionalized account of the slave who led an 1831 uprising against white slaveholders in Virginia. This novel is unusual in that the story is told from the point of view of a black man. This bestselling work was praised by some and bitterly criticized by others, who thought that it glorified a mass murderer. It won the United States' highest literary award, the Pulitzer Prize, in 1968.

Styron has continued to write. His novel *Sophie's Choice,* about a woman who is forced by the Nazis to choose which of her two children must live and which must die, was made into an award-winning film. His most recent work, *A Tidewater Morning, Three Tales from Youth,* is a collection of three stories set in the Tidewater area of Virginia.

MUSICIANS

Virginia celebrates music all year. The famous Jazz Festival in Hampton is one of the most popular jazz celebrations in the world. On a smaller scale is the Old Fiddler's Convention, held in the small western Virginia town of Galax each August. This is the oldest and largest fiddler's convention in the world. In addition to fiddlers, players of mandolins, banjos, dulcimers and autoharps perform along with traditional flat-footed dancing. The audience gets involved, dancing and clapping to the music.

Musicians at Galax's Old Fiddlers' Convention.

Ella Fitzgerald rehearses for a jazz concert in 1952.

Lexington's "Friday's Alive" festival has concerts both indoors and outdoors in August. Wolf Trap Farm Park in northern Virginia hosts outdoor concerts all summer. All kinds of music—classical, jazz, and popular—is played there. The casual atmosphere of the concerts in their beautiful outdoor setting draws families to picnic, dance, and play while the music is being performed.

One of the most famous American singers was from Virginia. Ella Fitzgerald was born in 1918 in Newport News. Her father deserted them, and her mother married another man when Ella was three. The family moved to New York. Ella did not get along with her stepfather, and after her mother died when Ella was fifteen, she lived on the streets as a runaway. She was discovered by bandleader Chick Webb in 1934 when she won an amateur contest at the famous Apollo Theater in Harlem. She joined Webb's band. She sang in the popular jazz style known as "scat singing" and also recorded the works of American composers Irving Berlin, Cole Porter, and the Gershwins. Her "song-books," multi-volume recordings, are classics of the jazz era. She won countless awards, including eight Grammies, the American Music Award, and the Kennedy Center Honors Award.

Toward the end of her life, Ella Fitzgerald continued to perform, but she was in poor health and nearly blind. Both her legs were amputated in 1994 because of complications from diabetes. America's "First Lady of Song" continued to be active, granting interviews and inspiring younger artists until her death in June l996.

Just as Ella Fitzgerald was one of America's most important jazz artists, one of the most important country singers was a native of Virginia. Patsy Cline was born in Winchester, Virginia, in 1932. She died in a plane crash in 1963 that also took the lives of several other country stars. Her records still sell well. Three of her records are among the top 50 country songs ever made, including number four, "Crazy," and number five, "I Fall to Pieces." The recently restored Kurtz Building in downtown Winchester is home to an exhibit honoring her, the city's most famous citizen.

ACTORS

Movie stars must love Virginia, because many of them move there after they become successful. Sissy Spacek, Robert Duvall, and

Christopher Reeve are among the many film stars who have been attracted to the beauty of the state.

One of the earliest theaters in America is Abingdon's famous "Barter Theater." In the nineteenth century, very few people went to see plays in Richmond. The actors were so desperate that they said that anyone who brought them food could stay and see the play. This strategy worked. A lot of people came to the performances. After a few weeks the actors went back to charging money. The people who had been to the play when they bartered (traded) food for entertainment remembered how much they had enjoyed the show, and now they were happy to pay money for the performance. Nowadays, the Barter Theater still puts on plays in Abingdon, but they charge money for admission, except when they hold food drives and ask people to bring a can of food to donate to the homeless.

Brother and sister Warren Beatty and Shirley MacLaine are very successful performers. (MacLaine is also a singer, dancer, and writer.) Both were born in Richmond, MacLaine in 1934 and Beatty in 1937. Warren Beatty has produced and directed films as well as acted in them, winning the 1981 best director Oscar for "Reds," which he produced, directed, and starred in.

Shirley MacLaine's first film appearance was in Alfred Hitchcock's "The Trouble with Harry." She went on to star in more than forty films. Although she won an Academy Award for her appearance in the 1983 film "Terms of Endearment," she is best known today for her books. In some, she talks about her belief in reincarnation. Her 1995 memoir *My Lucky Stars: A Hollywood Memoir* is more conventional, recalling the "good old days" in

Shirley MacLaine, author, dancer, singer, and film star, says of stage performance, "It keeps me alive."

Hollywood. She was honored in a tribute by the American Film Institute in 1995.

ATHLETES

Unfortunately for the sports fan, Virginia has no professional teams, although the Washington Redskins train in Virginia's Loudoun County. This situation may change in the future, however. Some people have been trying to move a professional baseball team to the state.

But there are other events the sports enthusiast can attend. Two Triple-A minor league baseball teams have their home in Virginia, one in Richmond and the other in Norfolk. There are also several very good hockey teams. And then, the waters of the bay, ocean, and rivers, and the artificial lakes of the Piedmont are the scene of sailing races and regattas throughout the year.

Virginia's horse country sets the stage for some of the most famous horse shows in the country. Fox-hunting is still popular, too, despite opposition from animal rights activists. Followers of this sport point out that they rarely see a fox, much less kill one, while hunting. They say they simply enjoy wearing the traditional costumes and riding their horses in the beautiful countryside with their friends.

Several important athletes are from the Virginia. These include the Washington Redskins' Gary Clark, and pro football Hall of Famers Willie Lanier, Fran Tarkenton, and Bill Dudley. Virginia's Mary Meagher Plant won two Olympic gold medals in swimming, and golfer Sam Snead has racked up an impressive number of wins, including three Masters titles, three PGA titles, and a British Open title. Many of these athletes are members of the Virginia Sports Hall of Fame, located in Portsmouth.

Virginia's best known athlete, though, is tennis player Arthur Ashe. Ashe fought three major battles in his life. He fought to integrate the white world of professional tennis, to rise to the top of the tennis world, and to defeat the AIDS virus. The first two fights he won; the third he lost.

Born in 1943 to a close-knit family in Richmond, Virginia, Arthur Ashe was an athletic boy who started playing tennis at age seven on blacks-only courts. Although he lost his first tournament, he quickly improved his game and discovered that he loved competition.

THE FOXHUNT

Sally Goldfarb grew up foxhunting. She belonged to the Pony Club, an international organization for children who like to ride horses. Many of Virginia's Pony Clubs are linked to local hunt groups. The children are supposed to ride in the back of the field so they don't get in the way of the more experienced riders, but Sally says, "My pony loved to hunt and I would often be seen hunting in the front of the field."

The rider who leads the hunters is called the Master. The Huntsman cares for the foxhounds, Virginia's state dog. He (or she) is familiar with the behavior of the hounds and can recognize from their barks and howls when they have found a fox. He blows a signal on a horn to alert the other hunters. Then there is an exciting chase across country, with hounds and horses leaping over fences and hedges, wading across streams, and galloping over fields. If the hounds get distracted by the scent of another animal, like a deer, the Whipper-In cracks a whip in the air. The loud sound reminds the dogs that they are in the business of hunting a fox, not a deer, and they usually return to their task. When the fox "goes to ground"—down its hole—the hounds are called back and the fox is left to recover from a hard day.

Many tennis clubs in Virginia didn't allow blacks to play on their courts, so young Arthur had to concentrate on out-of-state matches. Traveling far from home was a hardship for the teenager, whose mother had died when he was six, and who was close to his father and younger brother. But he persisted, and when he was seventeen became the youngest champion of the American Tennis Association, the largest all-black tennis organization in the country. In 1965, he was named the best college player, black or white, in the United States.

Arthur Ashe was invited to play in the South African Open in 1973. He wanted to compete in this important tournament, but the laws of South Africa prohibited him from playing in public except as an "honorary white." He refused, saying he would not deny his heritage. The South Africans were so eager to see him that they accepted his conditions.

Two years later, Arthur Ashe won the Wimbledon open and was the number one player in the world. He won this title by defeating the much younger and stronger Jimmy Connors, using his experience and intelligence to out-think him on the court.

Arthur Ashe had several heart attacks and had major heart surgery twice. During one of these operations he received blood tainted with the HIV virus. After a courageous battle with AIDS, Arthur Ashe died in 1993.

After his death, the city of Richmond ordered a statue of their most famous athlete. It stood for a short time on Monument Avenue, a street lined by statues of Confederate generals, and then was moved to the Black Athletes' Hall of Fame, also in Richmond, which Ashe helped found.

6 EXPLORING VIRGINIA

Chincoteague Island

Virginia's natural beauty, historic importance, and location make it a fascinating and exciting place to visit. Tourists bring in a lot of money, but Virginians are protective of their state. When the Walt Disney company wanted to locate a theme park in northern Virginia, residents blocked its construction, saying that it would damage the environment and ruin the historical nature of the area.

About 50,000 tourists visit Virginia each year. Let's take a mini-tour ourselves, starting on the Eastern Shore and working our way to the mountains of the west.

THE EASTERN SHORE

The Eastern Shore can be reached from the mainland by the twenty-three-mile Chesapeake Bay Bridge-Tunnel. This is the longest combination bridge and tunnel in the world and runs from Norfolk to the southern tip of peninsula. You can stop along the bridge to watch seagulls from a special pier, to fish, to shop for souvenirs, or to look through the telescopes mounted at the stopping areas.

Once on the Eastern Shore, nature is the biggest attraction. Assateague Island can be reached by bridge from Chincoteague. Much of its Wildlife Refuge is off-limits to the general public, but there is still a lot to see.

The streets of tiny Tangier Island, off the Eastern Shore, are so narrow that cars can't fit down them, and the island's eight hundred residents get around mainly by bicycle. Most of the

Tangier Island is so low that the graves in the cemetery are raised above the ground to keep coffins from washing away at high tide.

PONY PENNING WEEK

Assateague is the largest island off Virginia's Eastern Shore, but no people live there. It is a wildlife refuge, inhabited by birds, small mammals, and wild ponies.

No one knows how the ponies got to Assateague. They are similar to horses found on the Outer Banks of the Carolinas and to the mustang, which are known to have descended from Spanish horses. They all share certain characteristics, including having one fewer vertebrae (bones of the spinal column) than standard horses. So the ponies are most likely of Spanish origin. How did they get to the island, though?

It is possible that the ancestors of the Assateague ponies escaped from early Spanish explorers. But some people think that they are the descendants of horses who were blinded so that they would not be too frightened to work in the gold mines the Spanish hoped to find in the Americas. A ship carrying mine ponies was wrecked off the Eastern Shore in 1820, and it is possible that some of them swam to the island. They then would have interbred with the descendants of horses brought to the island by the British in the 1600s.

For most of the year the ponies live peacefully, disturbed only by an occasional human visitor. But once a year, during the last week of July (locally called "Pony Penning Week"), many of the ponies are rounded up and made to swim across the narrow channel to Chincoteague Island. There, the foals are auctioned off. The money raised benefits the Chincoteague Fire Department, which owns the herd. Both local people and tourists go to see the small horses and to bid on them. The horses that are not sold swim back to Assateague.

Some animal-rights activists object to this tradition. They say that the animals are unaccustomed to humans and are terrified at being made to swim, which is not a natural activity for horses. But supporters of Pony-Penning Week point out that if the ponies are allowed to reproduce without any kind of control, there will soon be too many of them for Assateague to support. By removing some of the ponies, all of them will be more healthy.

island's inhabitants (originally from Cornwall, Great Britain) make their living by fishing and live in charming old Victorian houses. The island has been isolated through the centuries. In fact, until recently the inhabitants had so little contact with the outside world that they spoke in seventeenth-century English!

The small towns up and down the peninsula offer beautiful scenery, restaurants specializing in seafood, and shops selling local arts and crafts.

THE TIDEWATER

Williamsburg, Jamestown, and Yorktown, together making up the "Historic Triangle," are a natural draw for the history buff. Williamsburg is visited the most.

In the 1920s, the millionaire John D. Rockefeller became interested in this historic site, which at the time had fallen into disrepair. He founded an organization dedicated to restoring much of the town to its original form, to be used for teaching American history. Now eighty-eight buildings have been returned to their original appearance. These include private homes, the governor's mansion, stores, and inns. Guides, some of them children, wear colonial clothes. They lead tourists through the reconstructed section, talking about the history of the Virginia Colony. Hands-on crafts demonstrations allow visitors to make soap, candles, pots, and other materials using colonial technology. Colonial Williamsburg is an important source of information about the lives of slaves and free blacks, who made up half the town's residents in the colonial era. Archaeologists are still digging at Williamsburg, and

Reconstructed Jamestown. This colony was settled thirteen years before the Pilgrims landed at Plymouth Rock.

each year find more fascinating artifacts that tell them about life in the American Colonies.

Jamestown, site of the first colonial settlement, has suffered even more than Williamsburg from the passage of time. Only one structure is left standing. But the recreated Powhatan Indian Village has

PLACES TO SEE

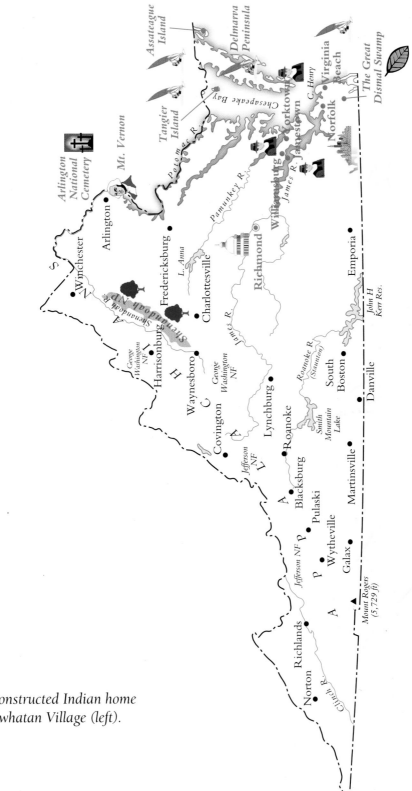

A reconstructed Indian home at Powhatan Village (left).

Assateague Island

Delmarva Peninsula

The Great Dismal Swamp

Chesapeake Bay

Tangier Island

C. Henry

Yorktown

Virginia Beach

Jamestown

Norfolk

Williamsburg

Potomac R.

Pamunkey R.

James R.

Mt. Vernon

Arlington National Cemetery

Arlington

Winchester

Fredericksburg

L. Anna

Charlottesville

Richmond

Emporia

John H Kerr Res.

Shenandoah R

Shenandoah NP

Harrisonburg

George Washington NF

Waynesboro

George Washington NF

James R.

Roanoke R. (Staunton)

South Boston

Danville

Covington

Lynchburg

Roanoke

Smith Mountain Lake

Martinsville

Jefferson NF

Blacksburg

Pulaski

Wytheville

Galax

Mount Rogers (5,729 ft)

Richlands

Norton

Clinch R.

many activities showing what life was like in the small Indian settlements.

Visitors also flock to the many beaches of the Tidewater. Virginia Beach was built about 1900 to attract tourists, and in the summer its twenty-nine miles of beaches are dotted with sunbathers. The warm water is perfect for swimming, surfing, and snorkeling.

Norfolk's bustling shipyards are fascinating to anyone interested in warships or the ocean. The national maritime center Nauticus, which opened in 1994, has hundreds of hands-on exhibits, theaters, and displays.

The Great Dismal Swamp, south of Norfolk, is a welcome break from the hustle of the city. Most of the swamp is a wildlife refuge where, according to one observer, the "water-snakes glide, the great trees add another ring, the insects rise at sundown, and the most exciting event of the day is photosynthesis." The swamp is home to a very unusual tree, the cypress. It has adapted to its conditions by growing long, skinny roots that come out of water, with the main part of the tree perched on top of them. These roots help it stay upright in the mud.

The outdoor sports of hunting and fishing also attract many visitors. Although the days when a hunter needed five or six dogs working together to retrieve his catch are gone, there are still abundant gamebirds and fish along the coast.

The northern part of the Tidewater holds attractions for many tourists who come to see Washington. Thousands each year visit Arlington National Cemetery, the nation's largest military cemetery and the site of the graves of President John F. Kennedy and his brother, Robert Kennedy, and of the Tomb of the Unknown

AN AMERICAN ORIGINAL: THE CHESAPEAKE BAY RETRIEVER

Only one breed of sporting dog comes from America: the Chesapeake Bay retriever. No one is sure of the "Chessie's" ancestry. Its main stock is some kind of retriever, with a mixture of several other breeds.

A favorite story of the retriever's origin is that two dogs, rescued from a wrecked English ship in 1807, were bred to produce the first of this breed. It is more likely that hunters living along the Chesapeake Bay carefully bred this dog to suit their purposes. And the dog is perfect for anyone hunting the many ducks of the Chesapeake Bay. It is large and devoted to retrieving; it doesn't seem to mind being in icy cold water; and its brown color blends into the surroundings, making it difficult for ducks to spot.

The Chessie is related to the Labrador, although it is more long-legged and slender than its cousin. The biggest difference, however, is in the coat: The Chesapeake Bay Retriever has a double coat that is woolly and coarse, and practically waterproof. A Chessie can spend a long time in water just above the freezing point, then come out, give itself one good shake, and be dry.

Very few people along the Chesapeake rely on hunting for their food any more, yet the breed is still very popular. Chessies are intelligent and loyal to their owners. Their intelligence, though, means that they often get bored and can get into all sorts of mischief if left alone for long periods of time.

Soldier. The Pentagon, which houses the U.S. Department of Defense, is also located in Arlington.

A sign on the outskirts of Winchester, a suburb of Washington, says, "Welcome to the Apple Capital of the World." There are many orchards in the area, and the oldest wealth in the city is found among the orchardists. So it is no surprise that each May, Winchester hosts one of the oldest celebrations in Virginia, the Shenandoah Apple Blossom Festival. Highlights of the festival are a fifty-float parade and the election of an apple-blossom queen. There is also the Fire Fighters' Parade, which is the largest display of fire-fighting equipment in the country. Sally Goldfarb, a native of Winchester, calls the festival a "huge deal—as soon as it's over the town starts planning for the next one. My cousin was Miss Apple Blossom, which is a qualifying title for the Miss Virginia pageant. I was Miss Gainesboro Fire Company!"

THE PIEDMONT

Virginia's capital city, Richmond, is in the eastern part of the Piedmont. The city was founded in 1682 and became the state's capital in 1780. It was also the capital of the Confederacy during the Civil War. It is now the third-largest city in the state (after Virginia Beach and Norfolk).

For Kapanga Kasongo, the most fascinating section of Richmond

The Marine Corps Memorial in Arlington National Cemetery is often referred to as the "Iwo Jima Monument," after a famous battle in the South Pacific during World War II.

TEN LARGEST CITIES

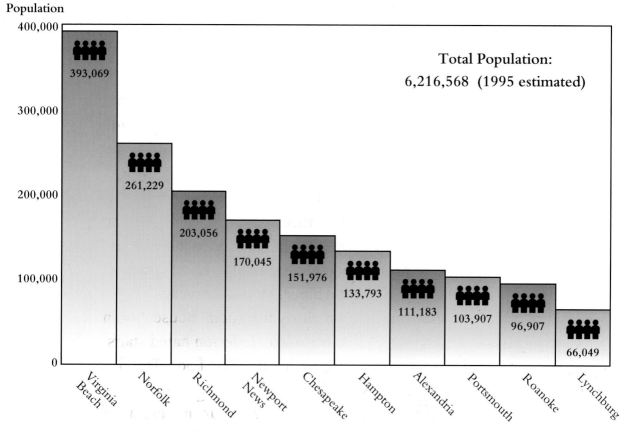

Population

Total Population:
6,216,568 (1995 estimated)

Virginia Beach	393,069
Norfolk	261,229
Richmond	203,056
Newport News	170,045
Chesapeake	151,976
Hampton	133,793
Alexandria	111,183
Portsmouth	103,907
Roanoke	96,907
Lynchburg	66,049

is the Fan, where many historic buildings and art museums are found. He was impressed when an exhibit of African art came to the city and he took his three small daughters to see it. Thousands of miles from his native Zaire, his children could see art made by people from his homeland. He calls Richmond "a very enriching kind of city in terms of all it has to offer, for example, the arts. And in terms of activities, there are all sorts of things going on."

Certainly the historic buildings of Richmond are part of the enriching nature of the city. The state capitol was designed by

Thomas Jefferson and now houses statues of all eight Virginia-born presidents. Museums include the Museum of the Confederacy, Richmond's City Life Museum, and the Science Museum of Virginia, one of the largest science museums in the country. Here visitors can operate hundreds of interactive exhibits.

Also of interest is the historic business area of First and Marshall streets, the site of America's first black-owned bank and insurance companies. The area is known as the "Wall Street of Black America."

The city of Charlottesville, located in the Piedmont, owes its importance to its most famous citizen, Thomas Jefferson. He founded the University of Virginia in Charlottesville in 1819 and designed the buildings of the main campus. These gracious structures are similar to Jefferson's home, Monticello, which he also designed. Construction on the thirty-five-room house began in 1770 and took forty years to complete. Jefferson hated stairs, so he put all the important rooms on the first floor. The few staircases are only twenty-four inches wide!

Jefferson was an inventor as well as a statesman and architect and created many innovations in his home to suit his own tastes. For example, in those days, clocks had to be wound every day. Jefferson invented a clock that needed winding only once a week. He made a copying machine, with two pens joined together by a bar. When paper is put under both pens, a person can write with just one of them and get a copy of the paper right away as the other pen writes too. He also experimented with agriculture. His gardens are still planted with descendants of some of the vegetables he introduced there.

Monticello was so large that Thomas Jefferson worried food would cool off between the kitchen and the dining room. He had his builders install dumbwaiters (small elevators) and other devices to move the food around more quickly.

THE MOUNTAIN AND VALLEY REGION

The Blue Ridge Mountains are the main attraction in this part of the state. Ethel-Marie Underhill, who has lived in eight states and three foreign countries, calls this area "undoubtedly the most beautiful place we have ever lived." Susan McArthur agrees, saying that what she loves most about her adopted state is, "how beautiful it is physically."

One of the most spectacular attractions is Shenandoah National Park, whose lovely name comes from an Indian word meaning "Daughter of the Stars." In 1994, almost two million people visited the park. Many visitors participate in the conducted walks and tours offered by the park service to educate people about the ecosystem of the area.

Other natural wonders include the Cumberland Gap National Historical Park in the southwest corner of the state. This gap, or low spot in the Appalachians, allowed settlers moving west to get their heavy wagons to the other side of the mountains. The states of Virginia, Tennessee, and Kentucky meet here.

Adventurous tourists enjoy caving in the limestone caverns of this area. Limestone dissolves in water, and the many underground springs have carved out huge caves. There are also many waterfalls and mineral springs.

Roanoke is home to the Transportation Museum, which traces the history of the railroads. Old steam engines and cabooses are set up outside and can be explored inside and out. The museum also has a collection of historic cars—in fact, of anything dealing with transportation.

THE BIRTH OF A PARK

The area of Shenandoah National Park has been inhabited by people since the Stone Age. Early Indians gathered food there, although they probably formed no permanent settlements.

Europeans settled in the Shenandoah. The beautiful, straight hardwood trees provided building materials, and soon most of the original growth had been cut down. The land was poor for farming, and by the nineteenth century homesteaders had used up all the fertile land on the mountain slopes. The thin mountain soil was washed away by the farming and the increased population. Then many of the chestnut trees, which made up about 25 percent of the hardwoods in the region, were killed by a fungus in the nineteenth century.

Concerned with the destruction of this beautiful area, Congress declared that money be raised to fund a park. Virginia contributed more than $2 million to buy the property of the two thousand people living there. Although some resisted, eventually all of them moved away. The park was dedicated in 1936. Today Shenandoah National Park is starting to return to the condition it was in when Europeans first set foot there.

At sunrise, the haze that gives the Blue Ridge Mountains their name already hangs over the hills.

From history to music, scenery to seafood, foxhunts to ethnic festivals, and politics to art, Virginia has it all. The state's unofficial motto is "Virginia is for Lovers." Not only Virginians, but the many people who visit the state are bound to fall in love with it.

THE FLAG: The state flag, which shows the state seal on a blue background, was first adopted in 1931.

THE SEAL: Although officially adopted in 1931, the state seal was designed in 1776. It shows the Roman goddess Virtus, representing the state, standing over the fallen body of Tyranny. The goddess holds a spear and a sword. The fallen Tyranny holds a whip and a chain, and his crown lies on the ground nearby. The state name appears at the top of the seal; the state motto, "Thus Always to Tyrants," appears along the bottom. A circle of Virginia creeper borders the figures.

STATE SURVEY

Statehood: June 25, 1788

Origin of Name: Named by Sir Walter Raleigh in honor of Queen Elizabeth I, the "Virgin Queen."

Nickname: Old Dominion, Mother of States, Mother of Presidents

Capital: Richmond

Motto: Thus Always to Tyrants

Bird: Cardinal

Dog: American foxhound

Flower: Flowering dogwood

Shell: Oyster

CARRY ME BACK TO OLD VIRGINIA

James A. Bland wrote "Carry Me Back to Old Virginny" in 1875. It became the official state song in 1940. Bland, who toured Europe and the United States with minstrel groups in the 1880s, wrote some seven hundred songs, including such all-time favorites as "Oh, Dem Golden Slippers," "In the Evening by the Moonlight," and "Hand me my Walking Cane."

When Bland wrote the lyrics to "Carry Me Back to Old Virginny," he used some words that we object to today. In 1997 the state senate voted to retire the song. In the following version you will find suggested changes.

Words and Music by James A. Bland

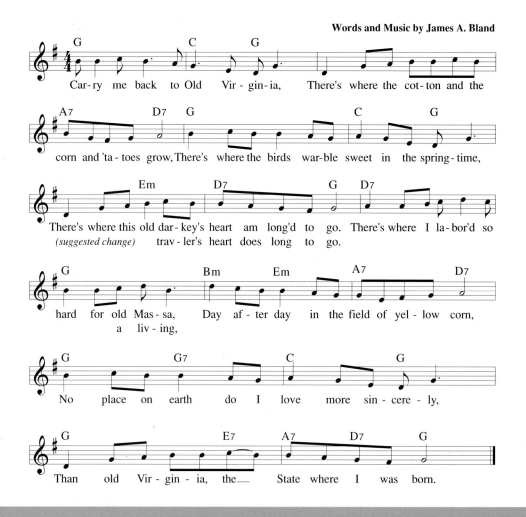

GEOGRAPHY

Highest Point: 5,729 feet above sea level, at Mount Rogers

Lowest Point: Sea level along the Atlantic coast

Area: 40,767 square miles

Greatest Distance, North to South: 200 miles

Greatest Distance, East to West: 470 miles

Bordering States: West Virginia and Maryland to the north, Kentucky to the west, and North Carolina and Tennessee to the south

Hottest Recorded Temperature: 110°F at Balcony Falls on July 15, 1954

Coldest Recorded Temperature: -30°F at Mountain Lake Bio Station on January 22, 1985

Average Annual Precipitation: 43 inches

Major Rivers: Potomac, Rappahannock, Rapidan, Anna, Pamunkey, James, Roanoke, Dan, Meherrin, Nottoway, Clinch, Holston, Powell, New, Shenandoah

Major Lakes: Smith Mountain, John Kerr, Anna, Claytor, Chesdin, Drummond, Moomaw, John W. Flannagan, Lake of the Woods, Monticello, Philpott, Leesville, South Holston

Trees: pine, birch, ash, oak, locust, poplar, sweet gum, black tupelo

Wild Plants: mountain laurel, rhododendron, azalea, Virginia bluebell, brown-eyed Susan, Queen Anne's lace, butterfly weed

Animals: white-tailed deer, black bear, fox, opossum, skunk, raccoon, rabbit, weasel, mink, bobcat, squirrel, beaver, river otter, wild pony

Birds: cardinal, pileated woodpecker, blue jay, robin, woodcock, tern, ibis, wild turkey, quail, mourning dove, swift, ruffed grouse, bald eagle, peregrine falcon, hummingbird, oriole, duck, snow goose

Fish: bass, bluegill, sunfish, perch, catfish, crappie, carp, trout, sea bass, striped bass, sea trout, bluefish, flounder, croaker, hogfish, menhaden

Endangered Animals: eastern cougar, Virginia northern flying squirrel, Virginia big-eared bat, Delmarva Peninsula fox squirrel, Dismal Swamp

southeastern shrew, piping plover, Shenandoah salamander, spotfin chub, yellowfin madtom, Roanoke logperch, Virginia fringed mountain snail, birdwing pearly mussel, James spinymussel, Appalachian monkey face pearly mussel, northeastern beach beetle

Endangered Plants: Virginia round-leaf birch, swamp pink, Peter's Mountain mallow, eastern prairie fringed orchid, small whorled pogonia

TIMELINE

Virginia History

c. 1500 About 18,000 Algonquian, Iroquoian, and Siouan Indians live in Virginia

1524 Florentine explorer Giovanni da Verrazano sails along the coast of Virginia

1570 Spanish missionaries found a settlement on the York River

1607 Jamestown founded

1614 John Rolfe exports tobacco from Jamestown

1619 The House of Burgesses meets for the first time

1619 First Africans arrive at Jamestown as indentured servants

1622 Native Americans of the Powhatan Confederacy attack English settlers along the James River, killing 350

1653 Virginia creates Indian reservations in Gloucester, Lancaster, and York counties

1667 A hurricane strikes Jamestown, destroying between 10,000 and 15,000 houses

1676 Bacon's Rebellion

1699 Williamsburg replaces Jamestown as the seat of Virginia government

1716 English settlers enter the Shenandoah Valley

1732 George Washington is born in Westmoreland County

1736 Virginia's first newspaper, the Virginia Gazette, is published

1755 George Washington appointed commander-in-chief of Virginia forces during the French and Indian War

1775 Patrick Henry delivers his "give me liberty, or give me death!" speech at Richmond

1775 Virginia's patriots seize Norfolk from the British

1780 Virginia's capital moves from Williamsburg to Richmond

1781 Lord Cornwallis surrenders his British army at Yorktown

1788 Virginia ratifies the Constitution and becomes the tenth state

1819 Thomas Jefferson founds the University of Virginia at Charlottesville

1831 A slave rebellion led by Nat Turner results in the deaths of about sixty whites before it is crushed

1859 John Brown seizes Harpers Ferry in an attempt to start a slave revolt

1861 Virginia secedes from the Union

1861 The first major battle of the Civil War is fought at Manassas

1865 General Robert E. Lee surrenders his Confederate army at Appomattox Court House

1870 Virginia re-enters the Union

1888 The world's first successful streetcar system begins operating in Richmond

1959 Integration of schools begins in Virginia

1969 Hurricane Camille causes damaging floods in central and western Virginia

1989 L. Douglas Wilder is elected governor of Virginia and becomes the country's first African-American governor

ECONOMY

Natural Resources: timber, limestone, dolomite, sand and gravel, quartzite, coal, oil, natural gas

Agricultural Products: hay, soybeans, corn, wheat, apples, peaches, grapes, strawberries, potatoes, tomatoes, peanuts, cotton, tobacco, broiler chickens, beef cattle, hogs

Manufacturing: transportation equipment, textiles, food products, electronic and telecommunications equipment, printed products, chemicals, drugs, robotics, navigation equipment

Business and Trade: wholesale trade, retail trade, transportation, government, banking

CALENDAR OF CELEBRATIONS

George Washington's Birthday (Alexandria) This celebration, held the February weekend of Washington's birthday, includes a Revolutionary War encampment and a parade with 200 floats, marching bands, and fife-and-drum corps.

Highland Maple Festival (Monterey) Held the second and third weekends in March, this festival features demonstrations on the making of maple syrup. There are also lots of maple-flavored treats to eat.

Dogwood Festival (Charlottesville) This two-week-long April festival celebrates the blooming of the dogwood trees with music, a quilt show, and athletic events.

Shenandoah Apple Festival (Winchester) In early May, apple orchards in the Shenandoah Valley are in full bloom. This weekend festival includes music, parades, rides, and a carnival.

Jamestown Landing Day (Jamestown) Held in early May, this celebration features sailing demonstrations and costumed actors playing the roles of Jamestown settlers.

Harborfest (Norfolk) This weekend festival in June celebrates Norfolk's place by the sea. Tall ships sail into the harbor, and there are sailboat races and fireworks.

James River Bateau Festival (Lynchburg) This eight-day-long festival in June features a boat race down the James River in old-fashioned traders' boats, or bateaux. Visitors can also enjoy music, crafts, and games.

Annual Pony Swim (Chincoteague) Every year in July, the wild ponies of Assateague Island are rounded up and swum across the channel to Chincoteague. Events in the festival include the auction of the ponies and a carnival.

Hampton Jazz Festival (Hampton) Great jazz sounds fill Hampton as some of the country's best jazz musicians play at this two-day July festival.

Virginia Highlands Festival (Abingdon) Appalachian culture is celebrated during this festival held in late July through early August. Appalachian music, art, crafts, and writings are featured. Hot-air balloons also make an appearance.

Old Fiddlers' Convention (Galax) This August celebration features bluegrass and fold music, as well as clogging and other old-time forms of dancing.

Publick Times (Williamsburg) Held on Labor Day weekend in September, Publick Times re-creates market days in eighteenth-century Williamsburg. Visitors can examine and purchase a variety of colonial crafts.

Virginia State Fair (Richmond) The State Fair, held every September, features entertainment, rides, exhibits on Virginia's farm products, and a pioneer homestead.

Oyster Festival (Urbanna) Visitors can try oysters prepared in a variety of different ways at this November festival. There are also tall ships, parades, and oyster boats to explore.

Grand Illumination (Williamsburg) The holiday season is celebrated in December as candles are lit and eighteenth-century decorations are hung throughout the town. Caroling, dancing, and fireworks are also part of the celebration.

STATE STARS

William Howard Armstrong (1914–   ), born in Lexington, is a writer of children's books. His most famous novel is *Sounder.*

Arthur Ashe (1943–1993) was, in 1975, the first African-American man to win the singles title at the Wimbledon tennis tournament. Born in Richmond, Ashe spent the last years of his life working to raise funds to find a cure for AIDS, with which he was accidentally infected during a blood transfusion.

Pearl Bailey (1918–1990), born in Newport News, was an accomplished singer and actress. She is most famous for her roles in the Broadway musical *Hello Dolly* and the movie version of *Porgy and Bess.*

Warren Beatty (1937–   ), a film actor and director, was born in Richmond. He received an Academy Award for directing the film *Reds.* His acting credits include *Heaven Can Wait* and *Dick Tracy.*

Richard E. Byrd (1888–1957) gained fame as an Arctic and Antarctic explorer. Born in Winchester, he was, in 1926, one of the first people to fly over the North Pole.

Warren Beatty

Willa Cather (1873–1947) won the Pulitzer Prize for her novel *One of Ours*. Born in Winchester, Cather's other books include *O Pioneers!* and *My Antonia*.

George Rogers Clark (1752–1818) was born near Charlottesville. A commander of Virginia troops during the Revolutionary War, Clark led daring raids into the Illinois country and captured the British forts at Kaskaskia, Vincennes, and Cahokia.

William Clark (1770–1838) was the younger brother of George Rogers Clark. William Clark, along with Meriweather Lewis, commanded the expedition sent by Thomas Jefferson to explore the Louisiana Territory in 1804.

Patsy Cline (1932–1963) was a popular country singer whose career was cut short by her death in a plane crash. Born in Winchester, Cline's hits included "Crazy" and "Sweet Dreams."

Ella Fitzgerald (1918–1996), the "First Lady of Song," was born in Newport News. Fitzgerald won eight Grammy awards for her jazz singing.

Patrick Henry (1736–1799) of "give me liberty or give me death" fame was born in Hanover County. Henry served two terms as governor of Virginia and led the fight to have the Bill of Rights added to the U.S. Constitution.

Patsy Cline

Thomas "Stonewall" Jackson (1824–1863), one of the most famous Confederate generals, was born in Clarksburg. Jackson earned his nickname at the First Battle of Bull Run when another Confederate rallied his own troops by exclaiming, "There is Jackson standing like a stone wall."

Thomas Jefferson (1743–1826), the author of the Declaration of Independence and third president of the United States, was born in Albermarle County. Jefferson was also an architect and an inventor. He designed his home at Monticello, many of the buildings at the University of Virginia, and the Virginia State Capitol in Richmond. Jefferson's inventions included the swivel chair and a clock that told the day of the week as well as the time.

Robert E. Lee

Robert E. Lee (1807–1870), born in Stratford, was the commander of the Confederate army during the Civil War. A brilliant military leader, Lee became the president of Washington College, today known as Washington and Lee University, after the war.

Meriweather Lewis (1774–1809), along with William Clark, was named by President Jefferson to explore the Louisiana Territory in 1804. Lewis was born in Albermarle County and served as governor of the Louisiana Territory after exploring there.

Shirley MacLaine (1934–   ) was born in Richmond. An actress, dancer, and author, MacLaine's films include *Terms of Endearment* and *Steel Magnolias*.

James Madison (1751–1836), the fourth president of the United States, was born in Port Conway. Madison is known as the "Father of the Constitution" for his part in writing that document. He also helped write the Bill of Rights to the Constitution.

Moses Malone

Moses Malone (1955–   ) was born and grew up in Petersburg. Malone was the first person to become a professional basketball player straight out of high school. A great jumper, Malone led the NBA in rebounding six times.

Cyrus Hall McCormick (1809–1884), born in Rockbridge County, revolutionized farming with his invention of a mechanical reaper. McCormick's machine allowed one farmer to do the work of five when harvesting wheat.

William Holmes McGuffey (1800–1873), a famous educator, was a professor at the University of Virginia. McGuffey wrote a series of books, known as *McGuffey Readers*, that were used to teach reading in American schools for many years.

James Monroe (1758–1831), the fifth president of the United States, was born in Westmoreland County. Monroe had also served as a U.S. senator, governor of Virginia, and U.S. secretary of state.

Pocahontas (1595?–1617), meaning "playful one," was the nickname of the Powhatan princess Matoaka. According to legend, Pocahontas saved the life of settler John Smith of Jamestown as he was about to be executed by the Powhatans. Pocahontas later married settler John Rolfe and became known as Lady Rebecca Rolfe.

Edgar Allan Poe (1809–1849) spent his childhood in Richmond and returned there later as a writer for a magazine. Poe is famous for his detective and horror stories, as well as his poetry. His works include "The Raven" and "The Pit and the Pendulum."

Bill "Bojangles" Robinson (1878–1949) was a well-known dancer and actor. Robinson danced in a number of Broadway musicals, as well as in several films. He was born in Richmond.

Kate Smith (1909–1986), singer and actress, is best known for her singing of "God Bless America." During the 1940s, Smith was called the "first lady of American Radio." She was born in Greenville.

Kate Smith

Maggie Walker (1867–1934) was born the daughter of a slave in Richmond. Walker became the first woman bank president in the United States after opening a bank in Richmond.

Booker T. Washington (1856–1915) was born a slave on a tobacco plantation in Franklin County. Washington later founded Tuskegee Institute in Alabama, a college for African Americans, and was a leading spokesman for blacks. His autobiography, *Up from Slavery*, has become a classic.

Booker T. Washington

George Washington (1732–1799), the first president of the United States, was born in Westmoreland County. Washington led the colonial army during the Revolutionary War and served as president of the Constitutional Convention before being elected the country's first president.

L. Douglas Wilder (1931–   ), elected governor of Virginia in 1989, was born in Richmond. He was the first African American to serve as a governor in the United States.

Woodrow Wilson (1856–1924), the twenty-eighth president of the United States, was born in Staunton. Wilson also served as president of Princeton University and governor of New Jersey. He received the Nobel Peace Prize in 1919 for his work in helping to establish the League of Nations.

FUN FACTS

Norfolk's recycling program created "Mount Trashmore," a mountain of trash that was turned into a children's playground.

The Pentagon in Arlington, the main offices of the U.S. Department of Defense, has almost 18 miles of corridors.

Richard Henry Lee and Francis Lightfoot Lee of Westmoreland County were the only brothers to sign the Declaration of Independence.

The country's oldest sporting event is the Natural Chimneys Jousting Tournament, held every August at Natural Chimneys Regional Park. Contestants use lances to catch steel rings while riding on horseback.

The Memorial Day holiday originated when a group of schoolgirls began placing flowers on the graves of Civil War soldiers in Petersburg.

Virginia has more miles of trout streams than it has roads.

One of the best-loved of children's books, *Misty of Chincoteague,* written by Marguerite Henry, tells the story of the ponies along Virginia's Eastern shore.

William Henry Harrison of Virginia served the shortest term of any United States president. Harrison caught a cold on the day he was inaugurated and died of pneumonia a month later. John Tyler, another Virginian, then took over the presidency.

Bill "Bojangles" Robinson of Richmond was a famous dancer of the early twentieth century. He could also run backward very fast and set a record by running backward 75 yards in 8.2 seconds.

In a custom that dates back to the 1600s, Mattaponi and Pamunkey Indians still present Virginia's governor with a number of gifts every year instead of paying taxes. The gifts include three arrows; wild game such as deer turkey, and fish; and pottery and baskets.

In 1861, Wilmer McLean moved his family from the Manassas area to get away from the Civil War after his house was damaged in the Battle of Bull Run. The McLeans moved to the quiet town of Appomattox in south central Virginia. Four years later, Robert E. Lee surrendered to Ulysses S. Grant in the McLeans' living room.

Robert E. Lee's favorite horse, Traveller, is buried next to Lee's grave at Washington and Lee University in Lexington.

Endless Caverns near New Market include formations named Snowdrift, Fairyland, and Grand Canyon. No one has ever discovered the starting point in this maze of caverns.

The Blue Ridge Mountains are so named because, from a distance, the trees that cover them appear to be blue.

TOUR THE STATE

Arlington National Cemetery (Arlington) This cemetery for the nation's military dead is an impressive sight, with row upon row of simple white headstones. The cemetery also contains the grave of John F. Kennedy, the Tomb of the Unknown Soldier, and Arlington House, Robert E. Lee's home before the Civil War.

Manassas National Battlefield (Manassas) The site of the first major battle of the Civil War has been preserved and looks much like it did in 1861.

Mount Vernon (Mount Vernon) George Washington acquired this plantation house on the Potomac River in 1754. Today the mansion has been restored to look as it did in the last year of Washington's life.

Chincoteague National Wildlife Refuge (Chincoteague) Visitors can view the many birds that inhabit the refuge from the Wildlife Loop, a 3.5-mile trail for cars and bicycles. Special bus tours go into areas of the refuge not open to cars.

Stratford Hall Plantation (Stratford) Built in the 1730s, Stratford Hall was the birthplace of Robert E. Lee. The plantation grounds include woods, gardens, and cultivated fields, all restored to look as they did in the early 1800s.

The Museum of the Confederacy (Richmond) Collections at this museum include equipment and clothing that belonged to Robert E. Lee, "Stonewall" Jackson, and other Confederate leaders.

Colonial Williamsburg Historical Area (Williamsburg) This re-creation of the eighteenth-century town includes the governor's palace, the Capitol, the courthouse, and numerous houses and taverns.

Jamestown Settlement (Jamestown) Costumed guides explain life in this reproduction of Virginia's earliest settlement. The ships that brought the first settlers and a Powhatan Indian village are also re-created.

Yorktown Victory Center (Yorktown) This museum of the American Revolution includes a Continental Army camp and a timeline walkway called "Road to Revolution."

Mariners' Museum (Newport News) Visitors can explore the history of humans on the sea, including special exhibits on the Civil War ironclad ship the *Monitor* and carved figureheads from sailing ships.

Nauticus, The National Maritime Center (Norfolk) Shipbuilding, environmental science, and the U.S. Navy are only a few of the maritime subjects that can be explored at Nauticus. Visitors can take the Virtual Adventures submarine ride or command a navy ship in a battle simulation.

Norfolk Naval Base (Norfolk) Visitors can take a guided bus tour of the base, home port to more than 100 navy ships. Some ships are open to the public on weekends.

Children's Museum of Virginia (Portsmouth) Lots of hands-on exhibits at this museum provide fun learning experiences for both kids and adults.

Virginia Marine Science Museum (Virginia Beach) Visitors can explore a Chesapeake Bay habitat through an aquarium exhibit that includes turtles, flounders, and sharks. Other exhibits allow visitors to create a fish on a computer and take a walk over a salt marsh.

Appomattox Court House National Historical Park (Appomattox) This village of 27 buildings has been restored to look as it did in 1865 when Confederate General Robert E. Lee surrendered his army to Union General Ulysses S. Grant.

Monticello (Charlottesville) Thomas Jefferson designed Monticello and lived there from 1770 until his death in 1826. The grounds include vineyards, an orchard, and a garden like that kept by Jefferson.

Booker T. Washington National Monument (Roanoke) This site re-creates the daily life Washington would have known in his early years as a slave on a small tobacco plantation in Virginia.

Virginia Museum of Natural History (Martinsville) Visitors can see a computer-animated triceratops as well as other exhibits showcasing Virginia's natural history.

Pocahontas Exhibition Coal Mine (Pocahontas) This exhibition coal mine explains the history of coal mining in the region and includes demonstrations of coal cutting and blasting.

Cumberland Gap National Historical Park (Ewing) The road that cuts through the park closely follows that blazed by Daniel Boone. Hiking trails and paved roads lead to scenic overlooks.

Natural Bridge (Natural Bridge) One of the Seven Natural Wonders of the World, the Natural Bridge is a limestone arch 90 feet long and 215 feet high.

Museum of American Frontier Culture (Staunton) Seventeenth- and eighteenth-century working farms from England, Ireland, and Germany are re-created here to show their influence on American frontier farms.

Luray Caverns (Luray) Caverns here range from 30 to 140 feet high and include gigantic rock formations. The Stalacpipe Organ uses stalactites to create music.

Shenandoah National Park (Front Royal) Hundreds of miles of hiking paths and the breathtaking Skyline Drive highlight this beautiful national park.

FIND OUT MORE

If you would like to learn more about Virginia, look for the following titles in your library, bookstore, or video store.

BOOKS

Fradin, Dennis B. *From Sea to Shining: Virginia.* Chicago: Childrens Press, 1992.

Fritz, Jean. *The Double Life of Pocahontas.* New York: Putnam, 1983. (A factual account of the life of Pocahontas both before and after the settlers' arrival.)

Henry, Marguerite. *Misty of Chincoteague.* Chicago: Rand McNally, 1947. (The award-winning story of two children who buy a foal at the Chincoteague pony roundup.)

McNair, Sylvia. *America the Beautiful: Virginia.* Chicago: Childrens Press, 1989.

Sirvaitis, Karen. *Virginia.* Minneapolis: Lerner, 1991.

Stapen, Candyce H. *Virginia: Family Adventure Guide.* Old Saybrook, CT: The Globe Pequot Press, 1995. (A guidebook that provides historic background and discusses places and activities likely to appeal to young people.)

Virginia Festival Fun for Kids! Atlanta, Georgia: Carole Marsh Books, Gallopade, 1994.

Virginia Jeopardy! Answers and Questions about our State. Atlanta, Georgia: Carole Marsh Books, Gallopade, 1994.

WEBPAGE

http://dit1.state.va.us
Frequently updated, this page is run by the Virginia Board of Tourism.

Your school librarian can help you find the CD-ROMs, videos, videodiscs, and computer software listed here.

CD-ROMS

United States Geography: The Southeast. Clearvue/eav, Chicago, IL.

Virginia Facts and Factivities. Carole Marsh Books, Gallopade, Atlanta, GA.

VIDEOS AND VIDEODISCS

The Early Colonists. United Learning, Niles, IL.
This video emphasizes the settlements in the Virginian Colony.

The Geography of the Southeastern States. Society for Visual Education.

The American Frontier: Jamestown. Society for Visual Education.

Rediscover America's State Capitals: Richmond, Virginia. City Productions Home Video.

Looking for America: The Southeast. Clearvue/eav, Chicago, IL.

SOFTWARE

Great American States Race. Heartsoft, Tulsa, OK.
This disk (PC or Mac) can be played at three different levels of difficulty.

INDEX

Page numbers for illustrations are in boldface.

Abingdon, 91, 125
African Americans, 36, 44-
    47, **45**, 54. 66, 67,
    68, 69, 84, 87, 93,
    95, 102, 111, 118,
    126, 127, 129, 130,
    131
Alexandria, 71, 110, 124
Algonquian language, 26,
    28
animals, 18, 114, 120
    deer, **13**, 18
    domestic, 107, 117, **117**
    endangered, 120
    pony, wild, 100-101,
    125
Appalachian Mountains,
    12, 16
Appomattox Court House,
    39, 136
Arlington National Ceme-
    tery, **78**, 106, **108**,
    133
Ashe, Arthur, 93, 95, 126
Assateague Island, 15, 98,
    100-101, 125

banking, 84, 111
beaches, 17, 106, 110
Beatty, Warren, 91, 126
birds, 18, 20, **20**, 117, 120
bird-watching, 15, 20, 134
Bland, James A., 118

Blue Ridge Mountains, 16,
    18, 113, **115**
Byrd, Harry Flood, 46

capital punishment, 57
capitol, **48**, 110-111
celebrations, 39, 67, 124-
    125
    festival, 15, **15**, 68-69,
    71, 109
    music, **88**, 88-89
Chapman, John Gadsby,
    *Good Times in the New
    World*, 24
Charlottesville, 111, 124
Chesapeake, 110
Chesapeake Bay, 21, 23
Chesapeake Bay Bridge-
    Tunnel, 98
Chesapeake Bay Retriever,
    107
Chincoteague Island, 15,
    96, 101, 125, 134
Civil War, 38-39, **39-40**,
    41-42, 133-134
climate, 16-18, 119
Cline, Patsy, 90, 127
coal mining, 63
Colonial Williamsburg, **22**,
    102-103, 125, 135
computers, **56**, 60
construction industry, 60
crime, 57-58

Cumberland Gap National
    Historical Park, 113,
    137

dinosaur, 12

Eastern Shore, 14, 15, 20,
    98-102
economy, 60, 61, 123
education, 55-57, **56**, 129
    African Americans, 44,
    45, 46, 84
    alternative, 57
endangered species, 120
energy resources, 63
environmental protection,
    98
equal rights, 45
ethnic groups, 68-69

fall foliage, 18
farming, 44, 58, 60, 61,
    73, 82-83, 86, 123
fish, 20, 21, 120
fishing, **62**, 63
Fitzgerald, Ella, **89**, 89-90,
    127
food, 15, 70, 109, 125
fossils, 12

Galax, 88, 125
geography, 9, 12-14, 17,
    119

regions, 14-16, 73-78
Gilmore, Jim, 57, 58
government, 50-53
    federal, 9, 50
    politicians, 53-54
    taxation, 57
Great Dismal Swamp, 14,
    106

Hamner, Earl, Jr., 87
Hampton, 44, 88, 110,
    125
Henry, Patrick, 34, 53, **54**,
    127
history, 121-123
    Bacon's Rebellion, 33
    colony, 9, 21, 30, 31,
      32, 33, 34, 36, 53,
      70, 102, 103
    Confederacy, 38, 76, 77,
      135
    Declaration of Indepen-
      dence, 34, 36
    Reconstruction, 44
    Stamp Act, 34
Holocaust, 87

invention, 82, 110

Jackson, Thomas
    "Stonewall," 67, 128
Jamestown Settlement, 29-
    32, 102, 103,
    103-104, 124, 135
Jefferson, Thomas, 9, 12,
    18, 29, 34, **35**, 36,
    66, 111, 128, 136-
    137
Jews, 71-72, **72**
jobs, 50, 58-63, 73
juvenile crime, 57-58

King, Martin Luther, 67

law, 50, 52, 55
    Constitution, 36, 44
    court system, 52-53
    crime, 57-58
    Jim Crow, 45, 46
Lee, Robert E., 9, 67, 128

Lynchburg, 110, 124
lynching, 46

MacLaine, Shirley, 91-92,
    92, 128
Manassas, 39, 133
manufacturing, 59, 60, 61,
    82-83, 123
maps, 19, 61, 105
Marshall, George Catlett,
    53-54
Marshall, John, 53
Mason, George, 36
McCormick, Cyrus, 82-83,
    129
Monitor and the *Merrimack*,
    38, **39**
motion pictures, 87, 91, 92
mountains, 16, 18
museums, 72, 106, 110,
    111, 113, 135, 136,
    137, 138
music, **88-89**, 88-90, 125,
    126, 127, 130

Native Americans, 12, 26,
    27, 28, 29, 30, 32,
    33, 34, 66, 68, 114
Nauticus National Mar-
    itime Center, 106, 136
Newport News, 110
nickname, 9, 117
Nobel Peace Prize, 54
Norfolk, 93, 106, 110, 124

parks, 89, 113, 114, 137,
    138
people, famous, 126-131
    actors, 90-92, 126, 128,
      130
    business and industry,
      82-84, 129, 130
    music, 88-90, 126, 127,
      130
    politics, 53-54, 127, 131
    presidents, 53, 111,
      128, 129, 131
    sports, 92-95, 126, 129
    writers, 84-87, 91, 126,
      127, 130

Piedmont, The, 16, 75, 76,
    93, 109-111
Plant, Mary Meagher, 93
plants, 18, 117, 124
    endangered, 120
    tobacco, 30-31, 58, **59**
    wild, 114, 119
Pocahontas, 30, 31, 32, **32**,
    129-130
Poe, Edgar Allan, 84-85,
    85, 130
poems, 42, 43, 86
police, 58
pollution, water, 21, 23, 63
population growth, 21, 47,
    110
Portsmouth, 93, 110
Powhatan, 30
Powhatan Indian Village,
    103, **104**

race relations, 44-47, 66-69
Radford, 46
recreation, 18, 106, 113
Richmond, 38, 56, 57, 58,
    68, 69, 71, 72, 84,
    91, 93, 95, 109-111,
    125
rivers, 16, 23, 119
Roanoke, 110, 113
Rockefeller, John D., 102
Rolfe, John, 31
Roosevelt, Eleanor, 84

schools. see education
Scottish-Americans, **69**, 69-
    71
sharecroppers, 44
Shenandoah National Park,
    113, 114, 138
Shenandoah Valley, 16, **17**,
    71, 109, 124
shipbuilding, 59-60, 106,
    136
slavery, 36-38, **37**, 44, 71,
    84, 87, 102
Smith, Captain John, 8, 30,
    31
Snead, Sam, 93
songs, 42, 118

sports, 92-95, 106, 126, 129
  foxhunt, 93, 94, **94**
storytelling, 28, 74-75, 84-87
Styron, William, 87

Tangier Island, 99, **99**, 102
television, 87
theater, 91
Tidewater, The, 14, 18, 76, 87, 102-103, 106, 109
touring, 63, 98-99, 102-106, 109-115, 133-138
trees, 16, 106, 114, 119
Turner, Nat, 37-38, 87

Virginia Beach, 110
Voigt, Ellen Bryant, 86

Walker, Maggie, 84, 130
Warner, John W., 54
wars, 9, 34, 36, 38-39, **39-40**, 41-42, 46, **108**
Washington, Booker T., 44, 130, 137
Washington, George, 14, 34, **35**, 124, 131
Webb, Chick, 90
Wilder, L. Douglas, 54, **55**, 131
wildlife refuge, 15, 98, 100-101, 106, 134
Winchester, 41, 76, 77, 90, 109, 124
Wolf Trap Farm Park, 89
Wyeth, N.C., painting, **83**

Yorktown, 36, 102, 136